Praise for *The Queen of Whale Cay*

"Summerscale has crafted a fascinating short biography from this wild, absurd and sometimes disturbing life. . . . Elegant and often hilarious."
—*New York Newsday*

"A rich and colorful tale." —*Detroit Free Press*

"Beautifully crafted . . . meticulously researched . . . A fascinating, hilarious, and deliciously subversive read." —*Literary Review* (UK)

"A perfect balance of sly sarcasm and genuine empathy." —*Des Moines Register*

"Summerscale must be applauded for introducing readers to a fascinating eccentric whose life emphatically reaffirms the old adage that life is stranger than fiction. Great stuff."
—*Daily Mail* (UK)

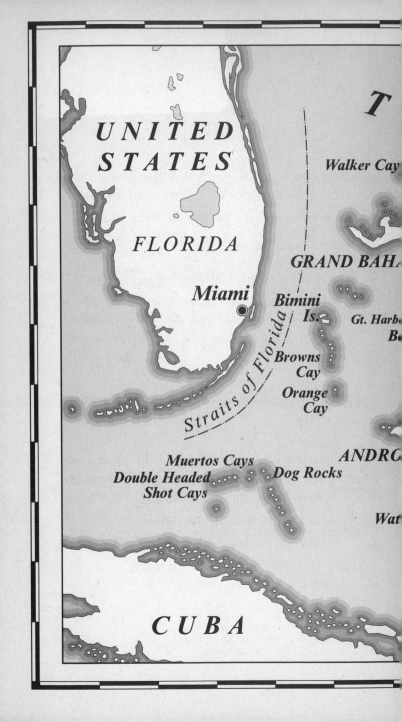

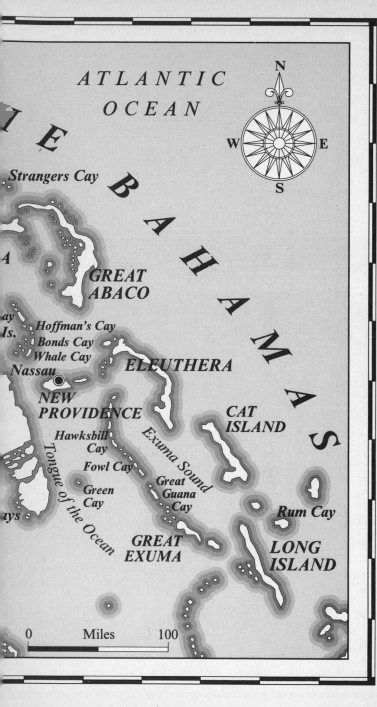

ATLANTIC
OCEAN

N
W E
S

THE BAHAMAS

Strangers Cay

GREAT
ABACO

ay
Is.   Hoffman's Cay
Bonds Cay
Whale Cay

Nassau   ELEUTHERA

NEW
PROVIDENCE   CAT
ISLAND

Hawksbill
Cay   Exuma Sound

Fowl Cay

Green   Great
Cay   Guana
Cay   Rum Cay

ays   GREAT   LONG
EXUMA   ISLAND

Tongue of the Ocean

0   Miles   100

PENGUIN BOOKS

THE QUEEN OF WHALE CAY

A resident of London, Kate Summerscale attended Oxford and Stanford universities and then worked at the *Independent* and the *Daily Telegraph,* where she was obituaries editor from 1995 to 1996. She is currently the editor of the *Sunday Review* for the *Independent on Sunday* newspaper.

THE QUEEN OF WHALE CAY

∞

KATE SUMMERSCALE

PENGUIN BOOKS

PENGUIN BOOKS
Published by the Penguin Group
Penguin Putnam Inc., 375 Hudson Street,
New York, New York 10014, U.S.A.
Penguin Books Ltd, 27 Wrights Lane, London W8 5TZ, England
Penguin Books Australia Ltd, Ringwood, Victoria, Australia
Penguin Books Canada Ltd, 10 Alcorn Avenue,
Toronto, Ontario, Canada M4V 3B2
Penguin Books (N.Z.) Ltd, 182–190 Wairau Road,
Auckland 10, New Zealand

Penguin Books Ltd, Registered Offices:
Harmondsworth, Middlesex, England

First published in Great Britain by Fourth Estate Limited 1997
First published in the United States of America by Viking Penguin,
a member of Penguin Putnam Inc. 1998
Published in Penguin Books 1999

1 3 5 7 9 10 8 6 4 2

THE LIBRARY OF CONGRESS HAS CATALOGUED
THE VIKING EDITION AS FOLLOWS:
Summerscale, Kate, 1965–
The queen of Whale Cay / Kate Summerscale.
p. cm.
ISBN 0-670-88018-3 (hc.)
ISBN 0 14 02.7613 0 (pbk.)
1. Carstairs, Joe 1900–1993.
2. Eccentrics and eccentricities—Biography.
3. Lesbians—Biography.
4. Motorboat racing—Great Britain—History.
5. Whale Cay (Bahamas)—Biography.   I. Title
CT9991.C37S96   1998
972.96—dc21
[B]   98–2806

Printed in the United States of America
Set in Perpetua

For my mother and father

We were so busy keeping you in existence that we had no time to grasp what you were.

Dolls: on the wax dolls of Lotte Pritzel,
Rainer Maria Rilke, 1913

CONTENTS

INTRODUCTION

At the end of December 1993 a letter arrived at the *Daily Telegraph* obituaries desk, where I worked, from a woman called Jane Harrison-Hall. She had noticed the name of her godmother, Marion Barbara Carstairs, in the death announcements column of the newspaper. Though Mrs Harrison-Hall had not seen her godmother for decades, she was writing to suggest she might be a suitable subject for an obituary; with her letter she enclosed copies of a few American newspaper articles.

No one on the desk had heard of Carstairs but when I looked up the name in the *Telegraph* library files I found a thick packet of newspaper cuttings, most of them reports of motorboat races. It seemed that M. B. Carstairs, born in 1900, had been famous in the 1920s. Always dressed in men's clothes, she had raced for Britain and established herself as the fastest woman on water. In 1934 she all but vanished when she left England to become ruler of the Bahamian island of

Whale Cay (pronounced 'key'). I wrote an obituary, giving it the heading 'Joe' Carstairs because this was the most widely used of the many names she took. The piece was published in the newspaper in January 1994.

A *Telegraph* obituary is formal in structure: it is anonymous, written in the third person and without overt commentary; it is topped, tailed and interrupted by facts and figures – the age at death, dates of birth, marriages, divorces, education, appointments, honours. This frame lends authority and authenticity, licensing the anecdotes, eccentricities and asides for which the *Telegraph* obituary is prized. In form, the obituaries imitate the unselfconsciousness of the figures they celebrate; in truth, they are mischievous and knowing. But the teasing is laced with affection – at the heart of these pieces is a lament, for a century and a spirit which is passing.

The spirit is embodied in the dotty dowagers and bristling brigadiers who people the obituaries column. These are the characters for whom the *Telegraph* obituary might have been invented, figures who are comically, heroically British. They are untroubled by whys and wherefores: they just are, and they just do. They persist in the face of disaster, of ridicule, of a radically changing world. The spirit they represent helped forge the British Empire; during the two world wars it made for astonishing bravery (the soldier who acted with 'reckless disregard for his own safety', in the words of innumerable military citations); and in peacetime it made for fabulous eccentricity.

Carstairs was all these things: blithe, bold, courageous, unselfconscious, imperialist, impervious to social change. And, like many of the eccentrics who appeared on the obituaries page, she was born to money: she could afford not to care. Yet Joe Carstairs was no dowager or brigadier – she was a cross-dressing lesbian whose fortune was made in the oilfields of America, in the years that the United States began to displace Britain as a great power. And though she didn't need to be, she was a relentless entrepreneur. Her ambitions were made the more astonishing by the fact that she was a woman, but they were over-reaching by any standards: fuelled by her money, she pursued a fantasy of autonomy and omnipotence, in which she was variously the fastest creature on the seas, an immortal boy and a great ruler of men. Her projects were so outlandish that they took her beyond fame and notoriety to obscurity.

An obituary aims to encapsulate how a person looked to the world, not how the world looked to them. It never presumes to enter the subject's head or heart, and so renders no interior life. It does not deal in meaning and motivation. After writing Joe Carstairs' obituary, I found that, for once, I wanted to fill in the delicate gaps that characterise obituaries, name the oddities suggested but left respectfully – or wryly –

untouched. I wanted to know why Joe Carstairs lived as she did, how the world worked upon her.

Apart from brief notices in the *New York Times* and *Motorboating* magazine, no further obituaries, to my knowledge, appeared. But in the weeks after the *Telegraph* piece was published, a handful of people who knew of Carstairs got in touch with me and I began trying to find others who remembered her.

Many of those who proved willing to speak to me about her were, I felt, motivated by the same curiosity that had engaged me. For all her directness of sentiment and action, Joe Carstairs was mysterious to those who knew her: she lived so much in the moment, with so little reflection, that her internal life was almost invisible. Carstairs did not look back and she never explained. She did not speak in the language of cause and consequence, meaning and motivation. 'I never felt anything *about* myself,' she once said. 'I was just *it*.' She believed the world and time exerted no force upon her, were merely backdrops to her performance. 'She made her life a series of scenes,' one friend told me. Joe did not see her life as a developing story, did not join up the dots – the obituary, by these lights, was a form that perfectly matched her. She would have approved of its strict adherence to fact and action: only a biography in pictures could have bettered its baldness.

But I wanted to test this version of her life. I started

by visiting Jane Harrison-Hall, the goddaughter who had written to the *Telegraph*, at her house in Hampshire. She was in her late sixties, and had known Joe only briefly before her flight to the Bahamas in the early 1930s. As a small girl, she had been driven around London in one of Joe's silver-grey Rolls-Royces. Mrs Harrison-Hall gave me lunch, pulled out her photograph albums, talked to me about her father and his three sisters, all of whom were friends of Carstairs. I sat on a velvet armchair, a dog lying before the fire, lights glowing, rain falling outside, the room lined with rugs and flowers, while I leafed through pictures of Joe Carstairs larking about on beaches and battlefields with Mrs Harrison-Hall's aunts. Before I left I used the guest bathroom, where I saw on the wall, like a giant clue, a photograph of a comic little man. He was Lord Tod Wadley, Mrs Harrison-Hall told me. The sealskin coat he was wearing had been bought for him by Joe Carstairs, as had his sailing cap and his handmade Italian shoes. It was some time before I grasped the significance of Tod Wadley.

Over the next year, in London, Lucerne, New York, Long Island, Florida and the Bahamas, I met several of Joe Carstairs' lovers, friends and employees, as well as members of her family and her Bahamian populace. I visited Whale Cay itself, hitching a lift on a small aeroplane; the other passenger was a man who had been called out to fix a generator for the couple who were the island's caretakers and sole inhabitants. After an hour or so the generator was fixed and we had to leave, the plane laden down with fish packed in ice. I had merely glimpsed the ruins of the kingdom Joe had built. As she had predicted, without her the island had returned to jungle.

I imagined that Joe Carstairs hoped on her death to be left, like the island, to return to wilderness. Yet I also knew that Joe had wanted her extraordinary exploits to be celebrated. As much as she sought exile, she sought recognition. I thought she would be glad to have a book written about her; it was a question of what kind of book.

There were many things that this book could or would not be. It would not be a book about lesbianism – Joe Carstairs was too singular and strange to be representative of anything other than herself. It would not be a tribute to feminist strength and success – after all, the principle by which she defined herself was male. It could not be a comprehensive or strictly chronological account – there were too many gaps in the available material. But it could be a book which connected Joe Carstairs to the century she spanned, a twentieth-century fable with a twist. And it could be a book which sought to find the stories which fastened together the scenes of her life. I wanted to map the island of Joe's fantasy. I realised that if I were to write such a portrait, the story Joe Carstairs wanted told and the story I wanted to tell about her would compete for precedence. I suspected I was going to have to work against the grain, extracting meaning where she had thought or wished there to be none.

My suspicion was confirmed when I listened to a series of tape-recordings she had made in 1975 and 1976 with a view to having friends ghost-write her autobiography. (Unsurprisingly, the ghost-written autobiography never came to fruition: Joe was a dominating figure, nowhere more so than in the facts of her own life, and one can only imagine what a tricky project it would have been to write her story while she lived. The tapes, though, are the source of many of the direct quotations in this book.) When an interviewer on the recordings asks Carstairs *why* she did something, she says flatly that she did it because she felt like it. Or she gets shirty.

'We want to find out what gave you that drive,' the interviewer patiently explains during an attempted discussion of her childhood.

'Why do you want to find that out?' Joe retorts.

The interviewer asks Joe how to reconcile two contradictory statements she has made.

'That's an enigma,' she replies.

'An enigma?' asks her friend. 'You think that's what you are?'

Joe firmly closes the subject: 'Yes.'

1

~~~~~~

I WAS NEVER A LITTLE GIRL

In 1905, or thereabouts, Marion Barbara Carstairs was thrown off a bolting camel at London Zoo. She was knocked unconscious; raw steaks were applied to her bruised head; and when she came round she had earned herself a new name, 'Tuffy'.

Joe Carstairs told a friend that this was the story with which her biography should begin. Her genesis, by this account, was of her own making: she was born not of human flesh but of her own will, and sprang forth fully formed, a creature of her desire. As she was thrown from the camel's back she threw off the feminine, proper names of the old century and of her family's choosing. Instead she took a name that assigned her to no one sex or time, marked her only with her resilience. To start her life story with this mock death and birth was to erase the first few troubled years of her existence, undo the bonds of parentage and gender, and claim the power of self-creation.

Later in life, she bridled at being accidentally referred to as 'Mrs' Carstairs: 'No man gave me my name,' she would bark.

'What about your father?' a mischievous friend once enquired.

'Don't talk to me that way!' roared Carstairs. She said of her father only that he was 'innocuous'.

If she was saddled with his surname, she swiftly loosed the first names of both parents from her memory. 'To this day,' she declared with some satisfaction in 1975, 'I don't know my father's name.' In the late 1920s she named her series of powerful motorboats Estelle, in honour of her mother. Many years later she discovered, to her amusement, that she had made a vengeful slip – her mother had not been called Estelle but Evelyn.

Yet, for all her fantasies of self-invention, Joe Carstairs did have parents, grandparents, a flesh-and-blood history.

Joe Carstairs's inheritance liberated her, of course, opened the world to her, fuelled her adventures and metamorphoses. But her perpetual supply of money robbed her of the opportunity to be – as her maternal grandfather had been, and as she longed to be – a self-made man.

Joe Carstairs's grandfather, Jabez Abel Bostwick, created the family fortune. Born in 1830 into a farming family in New York State, he amassed his money as treasurer to John D. Rockefeller's Southern Improvement Company. Rockefeller, Bostwick and their cohorts established an adamantine monopoly in the booming American oil and railroad industries of the late part of the nineteenth century. They first bought up most of their rival oil speculators in the choicest states, and then – by threatening to take their business elsewhere – secured massive rebates from the local railroad companies. These rebates enabled them to drive oil prices down and so drive other oilmen out of business.

In 1879 the Grand Jury of Clarion County, Pennsylvania, brought an indictment for conspiracy against the nine controllers of the Southern Improvement Company, Rockefeller and Bostwick among them. The charges were conspiracy to secure a monopoly in buying and selling petroleum and the use of fraudulent devices to control market prices of petroleum. The nine evaded arrest.

Jabez Bostwick had just built his family a stately five-floor townhouse on a corner of Fifth Avenue, New York, overlooking Central Park and near the residences of the other American oil tycoons. The house was equipped with elevators and electricity, and flanked by a stable. In the year of Jabez Bostwick's indictment the petroleum on which he had founded his fortune literally exploded in his face when he stepped down to the basement of his new house to repair a leaking gasoline tank. He survived the injury, again eluding disaster.

The Southern Improvement Company continued to flourish, and in 1882 was registered as the Standard Oil Trust, with nine trustees and capital of some $70 million. Its directors had exploited and outwitted the market economy, competing with such ruthlessness that they had all but destroyed the competition. Bostwick expanded into railroads.

Jabez's wife was Helen Celia Bostwick, known as Nellie. She was the only family member from whom Joe Carstairs acknowledged any emotional descent. 'Of all the grandchildren, she liked me the best,' Carstairs said many years later, 'and I was the most like her. I think I'm awfully like her, with my rages and violent tempers.' Nellie Bostwick was a fierce matriarch, even more stubborn and unyielding than her magnate husband. 'She was a wicked old lady,' recalled Joe with pride, 'rough, tough, she wanted her own way. She was a wonderful person . . . She had great power.' The stories Joe Carstairs told about her grandmother served to demonstrate her passion and her discipline. To calm her rages, Nellie would advance down the staircase at Park Avenue belting out operatic arias. A fervent supporter of the New York police force, when she spotted a policeman in Central Park she always halted her carriage to hand him a quarter.

Nellie had a habit of voicing the exact opposite of what she meant to say, to outrageous effect. Once, she was taking a walk with the eight-year-old Joe in New York — Nellie walked ten blocks a day — when they came across a man she knew who had recently suffered a death in the family: 'I'm so *glad* your sister is dead,' she told him.

'I thought this was marvellous,' Joe recalled. 'I broke up. I thought everything she did was marvellous.'

Jabez Bostwick died at his estate in Long Island in August 1892. The newpapers reported that he met his death while trying to rescue some horses caught in a fire in the stables. But rumour had it that he had in fact gone in to the blazing stables not to save horses but to salvage his favourite carriage: he tripped over its traces, hit his head against the wall and fell unconscious to the ground, where the fire overtook him. He left a fortune of $10 million.

In his obituary in the *New York Times* Jabez Bostwick was described as an active member of the Fifth Avenue Baptist Church who neither drank nor smoked, a prompt and punctilious businessman, a philanthropist with a 'staunch, unchangeable character'. The obituary hinted also at something beyond this god-fearing solidity: 'He was a restless man,' it noted, 'always entering into new ventures.'

Joe Carstairs was to inherit both the immutability

and the restlessness of her grandfather. And in the spirit of Jabez Bostwick, she was to harbour a passion for vehicles, for man-made power and locomotion, which more than once brought her close to death. She would have saved her cars or motorboats before any animal – she found horses, cats, dogs at best uninteresting, at worst repulsive. She invested her ambitions and affections in engines, fuelled by the oil her grandfather had drilled.

Jabez and Nellie had three children. The eldest daughter, also Nellie, was married at nineteen, lost a baby son at twenty-one, an infant daughter at twenty-four, and her husband at twenty-five; she remarried six years later and died in 1906, aged thirty-eight. The only Bostwick son, Albert, died in 1911 at the age of thirty-three – reputedly of drug abuse. The middle child, Evelyn, was the mother of Joe Carstairs.

In photographs taken at the turn of this century, Nellie Bostwick gives the camera an imperious, spirited glance; her younger daughter, Evelyn, gazes into the lens with a demure, pretty intelligence. Yet those who became entangled with Evelyn Bostwick saw her as fearless, capricious, a femme fatale. The disparity between Evelyn's portraits and her nature may be a mark of her complexity, or of her capacity to dissemble. 'She showed me there was such a thing as fear, which I have never felt since,' Joe said in old age. 'I've never been frightened of anybody except my mother.'

Evelyn Bostwick was born on 20 June 1872, and as a girl was known as Fannie (her first name was Frances). Much as her daughter Joe was to become a leading light of the London 'speed set', Evelyn Bostwick became a conspicuous member of the Long Island 'hunting set' and showed horses in Madison Square. At eighteen, she gave a hunt breakfast at the Bostwick townhouse, 'an event', according to the *New York Times*, 'which created much discussion in society'. That year, Evelyn started to dabble in drugs.

She also became betrothed to a young New Yorker, but their engagement was broken off shortly before the wedding day. In 1891, Evelyn announced that she intended to marry Captain Albert Carstairs of the Royal Irish Rifles, a Scotsman she had met on a trip to Europe. The wedding took place on her twentieth birthday, two months before Jabez Bostwick's death.

The marriage lasted a decade but little record of it survives. It is difficult to know whether it was Evelyn or her daughter, Joe, who effectively erased those ten years – and with them Albert Carstairs, Joe's father. Did Evelyn tell her daughter nothing of their life together, of him, of the circumstances of her birth? Or did Joe choose to forget it all? Something of Albert's life before his marriage can be gleaned from Army lists: he served in Egypt in the 1880s as a captain in the 2nd Battalion of the Royal Irish Rifles, and in 1891 was posted with the battalion to Malta. But he retired from the Army when he married in 1892, so his movements in the last years of the century are uncharted. As for Evelyn, vague anecdotes have been passed on about her serving as a nurse with the Red Cross in the Boer War and later racing a yacht against the Kaiser. Almost 100 years later, in the 1980s, her daughter Joe watched a videotape of *White Mischief* and remarked that her mother's world was similar to the jaded, dissolute expatriate society portrayed in the film.

It is not clear in which countries Albert and Evelyn lived, whether they even lived together. Evelyn was never a faithful wife, and perhaps we cannot assume that Joe was Albert Carstairs' daughter. The birth smacks of accident: the couple had been married for eight years when Joe was born, they divorced soon afterwards, and Albert seems to have made no attempt to keep in touch with his only child. He re-enlisted with the Army just a week before her birth. Maybe he was erased from her story because he abandoned her; or maybe she was illegitimate, and the identity of her father truly was a blank. If so, her claim in 1975 not to know her father's name carries an extra charge. Among Joe's collection of photographs was a blurred image of a fair young man, moustached, in uniform, marked 'Carstairs?'.

We do know that in 1900 Evelyn was living in London. On 1 February that year, she gave birth to Marion Barbara Carstairs at 115 Park St, Mayfair, a red-brick house in a newly built terrace. Just a few years earlier the street had been purged of its workhouse and public houses, to become one of the best roads in the smartest district in town. Mayfair was the nucleus of the London Season and – with the American Embassy in Grosvenor Square – a magnet for rich Americans. 'London's my town,' Joe said later. 'No question. Lord Fauntleroy, that sort of thing.' In Frances Hodgson Burnett's novel of 1886, Little Lord Fauntleroy, the son of an American woman and an English army captain, leaves the United States to take up the title and inheritance left him in Britain by his father. This was the land of Joe's lost father, too, which may explain why she was so anxious to lay claim to it.

Joe's inheritance was neither British nor aristocratic, but American and newly minted. And in the first few years of her life the fortune which was to sustain her was being reviled as the fruit of corruption. In 1902 a highly critical 'History of the Standard Oil Company' was serialised in the American magazine *McClure's*: it denounced the ruthless tycoons who had formed the company, Jabez Bostwick among them. And in 1905 the Reverend Washington Gladden, a pillar of the Congregationalist Church, refused a donation from Bostwick's partner John D. Rockefeller. 'Is this clean money?' he asked. 'Can any man, can any institution touch it without being defiled? In the cruel brutality with which properties are wrecked, securities destroyed, and people in the hundreds robbed of their little, all to build up the fortunes of the multi-millionaires, we have an appalling revelation of the kind of monster that a human being may become.'

Joe's mother, perhaps to counter her reputation in Europe as a 'dollar princess' – a princess of tainted dollars at that – somehow contrived to become a lady-in-waiting to Queen Alexandra, the wife of Edward VII. ('I think she *liked girls*,' Joe Carstairs remarked of Alexandra, though she seems to have based this belief solely on the fact that the Queen wore high collars and ties.)

By the time Joe fell from the camel – aged five or so – she had reason to feel orphaned. Her parents had divorced, her father had disappeared, she had been shuttled around Europe, between countries and nannies, and in 1903 her mother had remarried, producing a second daughter. Shortly afterwards, she bore a son.

Evelyn's new husband was Francis Francis, another British army captain (in the circumstances, it was fortunate that Evelyn no longer went under her first name, Frances). Her new children were Evelyn

Francis, known as Sally (born in 1904), and Francis Francis Jr, known as Frank (born in 1906). Joe did not care for her step-family, nor they for her. She derisively described Frank as 'a little girl's boy', though she admitted that because he was a boy their mother was 'slightly doting' with him. Joe said of herself: 'I was never a little girl. I came out of the womb queer.'

She was prone to scrapes and tumbles, sometimes wilful, sometimes touched with farce. The camel from which she was thrown at London Zoo bolted because a waiter flicked a napkin near its tail. If taken to a party dressed in a white frock, Joe would run outside and roll in the mud. She was lifted off the back of her Shetland pony, Nigger, by a bramble bush. 'From the time I learnt to walk, I ran,' she said. 'My mother said I was a bull in a china shop.'

Captain Francis disapproved of his wild stepdaughter. 'He thought he'd cure me,' recalled Joe, 'but he didn't.' This wildness, the sickness which was not cured, was even then a euphemism for her masculine behaviour. When Francis caught the little girl, aged eight, stealing his cigars, he punished her by ordering her to sit down in his study and smoke one. If you're sick, he said, go out, throw up and come back. Joe, who had been pilfering his cigars for some time, sat down and calmly smoked her way to the end.

Though Francis and Evelyn did not divorce until

1915 their marriage had long since crumbled. Evelyn had many affairs – it was said that the son of an English peer killed himself when she left him – and she took up and dropped her children as lightly as she did her lovers. Francis looked after his son and daughter in London, and when he heard that his estranged wife was planning a visit he would have Sally and Frank's nanny hide them in the attic. Once, Evelyn kidnapped Sally and Frank from the Coburg Hotel, and took them to her mother's house in America. 'Don't worry,' Nellie Bostwick told the distraught Francis. 'She'll get bored with them in time.' And so it proved.

Joe Carstairs had not even an anxious father to protect her from her mother's whims, and Evelyn, for all her negligence, seemed determined that her daughter should form no other attachments. According to Joe, Evelyn grew so jealous of a nanny to whom Joe was close that she fired her. This nanny, whom Joe had promised to marry when she grew up, for many years sent egg-warmers to her former charge.

Evelyn's vaulting moods were fed by alcohol and heroin. Within hours she could descend from brilliance to incoherence, her shimmer and charm dying into bitterness and loose cruelty. On the occasions that she was with her children she was often absent in spirit, the drugs rendering her glazed and vacant. Because of her unnatural volatility, Evelyn was both hated and adored by her eldest daughter. 'She was beautiful, she was bright, she was extraordinary,' Joe said, 'but she had this terrible thing of taking dope . . . She was unpredictable, to the limit of all.'

The young Joe Carstairs was in thrall to a wayward, mighty force which she had no means of resisting. In later life she would, very rarely, admit to having felt vulnerable. 'What was going to happen?' she said once. 'I never knew. I was a strong little brute but, you know.'

To survive, Joe constructed a fantasy of private power around herself, as if building a raft on the waves; this fantasy was to manifest itself throughout her life in her desire for walled, moated worlds – for boats and islands. One of her few happy memories of childhood was of sailing in her own dinghy on the sea near Southampton, armed with crackers and a jug of water. And she made little vessels from twigs. Even then, boats represented autonomy amid chaos. Who or what did she admire, a friend asked her, when she was a child? 'I didn't admire anything,' Carstairs replied. 'Except boats.'

All the stories Joe purveyed about her childhood were designed to illustrate her defiance and self-sufficiency, to prove that she was 'a strong little brute'. She did not cry when beaten with the back of a hairbrush, she said, because it would have made 'them' happy. She boasted of what a bully she was:

she particularly liked to stick pins in her baby brother Frank.

If Joe felt sorry for being cruel or naughty her penance was private and self-administered. She recalled that as a means of atoning for her misdemeanours she would run to a beach, lie in the sand and sweep her arms up and down to make the images of 'saints', or angels. On the heads of the sandy saints, as if to enact her own forgiveness, she drew halos. 'I thought I was helping,' she explained, and added, to remove any suggestion of compliance or virtue, 'helping myself'.

By her account, she was eventually deemed so 'dangerous' to her half-brother and half-sister that she was sent away to a boarding-school in America. It seems likely that she exaggerated the danger she presented in order to lessen the pain of her expulsion: her banishment, she tried to suggest, was not a mark of her powerlessness but of her power. 'I let them think it was a punishment,' she said, 'but I knew damn well I was going to have a bloody good time.'

In a one-page autobiography she compiled in her nineties, she effected this inversion neatly with a single phrase: 'Left family aged 11.'

2

A VERY HEALTHY LITTLE BEAST

In 1911 Joe Carstairs was wrapped up in a raincoat, driven to Southampton and put on an ocean liner bound for New York. The raincoat was the last vestige of the old dark world. Joe was entranced by the liner, a floating island, a complete, knowable world hemmed in by the sea. As she described it, the journey to America was a liberation, and Low Heywood – the girls' boarding-school she went to in Stamford, Connecticut – an idyll.

Joe spoke sparingly of her schooldays but with ease and lightness, as if this period of her life was so untroubled that there was little to say. She arrived 'a little dot of a thing' and won instant popularity by doing the seniors' French homework for them – she had learnt fluent French from a nanny. Even then, she recalled, 'I used to hold forth – God knows what about', and she relished the attention provoked by her 'frightfully English' accent. She claimed to be unable to count to ten and she could muster little concentration when reading, but she was a passable student and a good games-player. Joe loved wearing the school uniform. 'I was pleased with myself even then,' she said. 'I was a very healthy little beast.'

Ever mindful of her health, she ate oranges rather than sweets, and used her pocket money to buy boys' pyjamas and shoes. Her room-mate, Caroline Dubois, also liked to dress in boyish clothes. 'She was *so* good-looking,' Joe recalled. 'I tell you, we were just something.' Joe fell in and out of love with various girls, she said, but 'I didn't have any kind of sexual ideas . . . There wasn't time to do it at school, I had so many other things to do.' She revelled in being a scamp, a boy. Many years later, when she was middle-aged, she took two friends to see her old school. She told a caretaker they encountered there that she was a former student. To her delight, he explained that she must be mistaken as this had always been an all-girls' school.

Yet Joe's mother cast her shadow over these sunny schooldays. On the passage to America Joe had done her best to leave behind all the stuff of her past – her new-found happiness must have entailed a fierce act of will – but somewhere it lingered. 'I was frightened of what might happen,' Joe said. 'She was doping, I was enjoying myself to the full at school, terrified she was going to write and tell me to come home.'

For all her fears of being recalled by her mother, Joe saw her only once in this period – in 1915. That year,

Evelyn divorced Francis Francis to marry her third husband, Roger de Perigny, in the Catholic church in Warwick Street, London. De Perigny was a French count and a sub-lieutenant in the 19th Regiment of the French Dragoons. Joe adored him. 'He was marvellous,' she said. 'He was a boy.' What was more, he treated his stepdaughter as a boy, adapting his racing car, a Peugeot, so that she could drive it, offering her his cigars and introducing her to his many mistresses – once, Joe proudly recounted, he took her with him on a visit to a Parisian brothel. 'He was absolutely the greatest charmer of all time,' Joe said. 'I was like his son almost. He thought I was the end.' He may also have been the first man Joe met who was not under the spell of her mother. For once, Evelyn was the betrayed rather than the betrayer. She eventually left her third husband on account of his persistent infidelity.

During other holidays from school Joe sometimes stayed with her grandmother, Nellie, in New York. In his will of 1892 Jabez Bostwick, an ardent patriot, had stipulated that only those of his heirs resident in America should be entitled to a share of the fortune. Since he died soon after Evelyn's first marriage, this clause may have been designed to punish his daughter for marrying a Scotsman and leaving her country. But Nellie Bostwick, ignoring his wishes, had ensured that generous incomes were provided for Evelyn and her children. It was Nellie to whom Joe expressed her ambition to be a doctor. (Evelyn vetoed this: 'She was jealous of me, fundamentally,' Joe said.) And Joe begged Nellie to let her go to war. Nellie Bostwick, a woman of some influence as well as resolve, persuaded the American Red Cross to send her sixteen-year-old granddaughter to drive ambulances in France. In 1916 Joe, who had been shuttled back and forth between the Old and New Worlds since birth, crossed the Atlantic for the seventeenth time in not quite as many years; the ocean had come to seem her natural element, the liners the still centres around which her world turned.

Joe Carstairs reached Paris shortly before the Americans joined the Great War. Her mother was living in the city with a chihuahua which Joe described as 'a horror': 'He used to pretend he had heart trouble,' Joe claimed, 'by lying on his back with his legs up, and she used to feed him brandy.' While Joe idealised inanimate objects, investing them with the loyalty and innocence of children, she attributed to animals the treachery and guile of adults.

Joe moved in to an apartment in Montparnasse with four other ambulance drivers. The flat was cheap to rent because it had a glass roof, through which the girls could see bomber aircraft flying overhead. Paris was heavily shelled, Joe recalled: whole sides of houses fell down and people lay bleeding in the streets. She was driving an ambulance in the Place de la Concorde when an aircraft was shot out of the sky, to fall in the snow before her. She picked the pilot, a Frenchman, out of the wreckage and found he was dead.

In Paris she had her first sexual encounter, with a woman in a hotel room – 'I said, "My God, what a marvellous thing." I found it a great pity I'd waited so long.' She then became infatuated by Dorothy Wilde, a fellow ambulance-driver who shared her flat in Montparnasse. Joe and Dolly had an affair, and Joe was to cite Dolly as one of the four women who changed her life.

To those who knew her, Dolly Wilde was so potent, so unprecedented, that she seemed a character from a novel rather than from life. Like Joe Carstairs, she has not made her mark on history – she was a creature of the moment.

Dolly Wilde was born in 1895, to Willie Wilde and his wife, Lily. Oscar Wilde was her uncle, and after his death she was the only member of the family to bear his name (such was Oscar's social disgrace that his two sons took their mother's name, Holland). Willie, like his younger brother, was tall, fleshy and languid; he aspired – hopelessly – to Oscar's conversational and artistic brilliance, and died a drunk in 1899, when Dolly was four. Lily remarried. The only childhood memory Dolly relayed to her friends was of eating sugar cubes dipped in her mother's perfume.

Oscar died in Paris in 1900, exiled and reviled for his homosexuality, sick, broken and broke. Fourteen years later Dolly burst upon the Parisian scene like a resurrection. This resurrection, though, was marvellously inverted: her uncle had loved boys, she loved girls; she was the mannish woman to his feminine man. He might have stepped through a mirror to become her.

When Dolly died, young, her friends wrote down their memories of her, and in 1951 privately published their recollections in a slim paperback. According to Rosamond Harcourt-Smith, Dolly had 'the same oval face as Oscar . . . the same dark hair growing in a peak on the brow, the same long, boneless white hands'. Dolly was tremendously proud of her hands, their tapering fingers, their soft narrow wrists and palms; they were, another friend remarked, so white and perfect as to be curiously inexpressive. Alice B. Toklas, the lover of Gertrude Stein, wrote of Dolly's 'almost mythical pristine freshness'. Dolly had the hips of a boy, the shoulders of a man, and the grace and loveliness of a girl – she was once described as a statue made of gardenia petals, with two huge violets for eyes. 'Half-androgyne', said the great love of Dolly's life, Natalie Clifford Barney, 'and half-goddess'.

Natalie Barney, a rich American expatriate and patron of the arts, was the most famous lesbian alive; the writer Remy de Gourmont dubbed her *l'Amazone* after seeing her magnificent bearing as she rode astride through the Bois de Boulogne. Natalie Barney's Friday night salons, at which tea and chocolate cakes were served, attracted the celebrities of the day: Rabindranath Tagore, Paul Valéry, Proust, Gide, Eliot, Cocteau, Colette, Rilke, Joyce, Pound, Hemingway; before the war, Mata Hari rode naked at Barney's salon on a white horse wearing a turquoise-studded collar.

In Paris as nowhere else, a bohemian, sexually diverse society flourished, and many went there in search of freedom, of the mind and of the body. Dolly Wilde spun at the heart of this world, but Joe Carstairs was on the periphery. 'I was too nondescript,' Joe said. 'I was still in embryo.' To the Parisian sophisticates she was simply a stocky, gauche American girl, steeped in new money and unschooled in art or literature. Though Joe may not have been allowed to enter their circle, its example influenced her profoundly. She and others who spent time in Paris during the war were to create their own version of the Parisian scene in 1920s London.

Dolly introduced Joe to the excitements of sex and of intellect. 'I knew [her] *excessively* well,' Joe said. 'She taught me the elasticity of thought. She taught me to think.'

Dolly was known for her sparkling conversation. Yet Dolly's words, unlike those of her uncle, were evanescent, careless, utterly resistant to repetition or transcription. At parties, wrote Bettina Bergery, 'she scintillated with so many epigrams, all delivered at once – that no one had time to remember any . . . Her

28

words flew out like soap bubbles.' 'It was wit that was impossible to quote,' wrote Pamela 'Honey' Harris, 'the quickest, lightest, most extravagant nonsense, with no bounds, no inhibitions, and often no sense of suitability.'

Dolly never worked, never exerted herself; she moved languorously and was always late. She was fabulously indolent. She had, wrote Lorna Lindsley, 'a sort of elusiveness that made for laziness; she would not lift a finger, not even to beckon, but people came just the same . . . Dolly never "did" anything. She just *was*.' People came, as often as not, to confide in Dolly. She had a huge appetite for gossip, preferably of an amorous nature, and became a kind of voracious agony aunt. She would plot, intrigue, entertain, advise, chastise her friends and – ultimately – betray their secrets. 'Her discretion, it cannot be denied,' wrote Victor Cunard, 'was not as great as her capacity for amassing information.' Another acquaintance, Antoine Gentien, was less delicate: 'Friendship requires discipline, and Dolly had none.' Dolly loved to tease and mock, to watch her victims squirm. 'She was like a panther,' said Rosamond Harcourt-Smith, 'softness, grace, purrs and of course, claws.'

Once, when taken for tea in Paris by a rich American bachelor, Dolly had the waiter leave a silver salver of brioches on the table. She proceeded to cut off and swallow the little mounds capping each brioche, until eventually two dozen decapitated buns lay on the salver. Her host, having watched with mounting fury, paid the bill and reprimanded his guest. 'But they are the best part of the brioches,' Dolly protested, 'I didn't want the rest.' A friend asked her afterwards what had motivated this display. 'I don't really know,' said Dolly, 'but I think it was to reproach him for his riches.' Even she didn't know whether her gestures had meanings: she could see herself as a subversive performance artist, transforming social niceties into witty symbolic dramas, or simply as a wilful child unable to resist temptation.

Dolly's apparently beguiling inventiveness betrayed a profound boredom and disappointment: to be made interesting the world had to be transformed to fiction. Dolly Wilde was herself a literary allusion, a shimmering reference to Oscar. Her friends saw her always in relation to him, and subtitled their volume of tributes to her 'Oscaria'. Dolly was enchanted and ensnared by the memory of her uncle; she felt Oscar's spirit possessed her, compelled her. 'I am more like Oscar than Oscar himself,' Dolly would say. She went to masquerades dressed up as him. In a letter, she wrote: 'I *couldn't* resist the "bon-mot" which sprang to my lips (Oscar's lips after all!)' She adopted other guises too. Bettina Bergery described a typical Dolly Wilde performance, set in a small restaurant on the Quai de Voltaire:

Her face is exactly Aubrey Beardsley's drawing of Oscar Wilde. The others are talking, she is looking dully at an empty glass as she strips the leaves from a sprig she had taken from the flowers on the table. A tall red-headed boy comes in and recognises Victor [Cunard], who begins introducing. Dolly's eyes light up as she interrupts: 'Darling, you do introduce so badly, you don't know how to introduce at all: you just mention names he doesn't know, and that makes conversation so general!' Now she addresses the boy directly: 'Victor, you don't need to be told, is the White Knight from Alice in Wonderland, and this' – pointing her twig at Yorke, a golden-headed German – 'is Siegfried. It's not red wine in his glass, he only drinks blood, dragon's blood, that's why he is smiling at the impertinent things the canaries in the cage over the caissière's desk have been saying about us. He understands them perfectly. She' – the twig now points at Ruth Yorke – 'whose features are as taut as a red indian's, who knows what rites she performs when the moon is full. As for me . . . you should have recognised me first and rushed to me – even without my turban, because I am Madame de Staël. If you've forgotten my face you should have remembered my branch' – here she waves her twig – 'and my beautiful hand and forearm. "My only perfection", as you told me once. Well

I knew you immediately, you haven't changed a bit; you are Benjamin Constant.' Forgetting that Benjamin Constant [author of the novel *Adolphe*] had been covered with eczema as well as red hair, the red-headed boy is terribly flattered. Also forgetting he is a shy stranger, he has seated himself at the table without being asked. Lost in Dolly's eyes which grow more and more laughing and luminous, he is talking as he has never talked before. Luckily he has read *Adolphe* and is telling Dolly how strangely alike his own story is, only stopping to empty his glass again. Next morning he springs to his phone to call Dolly. But Dolly won't be awake for a long time and when she is, her telephone is busy. He goes to the Ritz, where she promised to lunch, but Dolly has forgotten her promise.

In flattering and wooing Joe Carstairs as she wooed the red-headed boy, Dolly taught her that by recreating herself in the image of a fictional character her gaucherie could be transformed to charm. Joe learnt her lesson. She never underestimated the powers a theatrical self could afford. Joe did not mention how she and Dolly parted. Perhaps Dolly abandoned her as easily as she abandoned the red-headed boy, and taught Joe another lesson: not to trust.

To fuel her relentless gaiety and invention, Dolly Wilde was to turn to drink, to opium and to cocaine, bought from the '*marchands de paradis*' on Parisian street corners. Like Joe Carstairs' mother, she was soon 'doping', and her life ended pathetically.

'Dolly Wilde, in life, was like a character out of a book,' wrote Janet Flanner, 'even if it was never written. On the street, walking, or at a Paris restaurant table, talking, or seen in the dim, sunset light of her rue de Vaugirard flat, remote in its inner court, she seemed like someone one had become familiar with by reading, rather than by knowing.' Joe Carstairs, for all her physicality and vigour, acquired something of this quality. She was not a literary, intellectual type; but she nevertheless gave the impression of being a fictional creature, a product of her own imagination, a being who 'just was'. Like the armoured goddess Athena, who emerged fully formed from Zeus's head, both Dolly and Joe strove to give the impression of being invented rather than born.

Joe, at seventeen, was dazzled by Dolly; she found her 'almost mystical'. Dolly was the first − or the second if we include Joe's mother − of the clever, glamorous, flighty women to whom Joe was drawn, women with a streak of cruelty and a well of unhappiness. This early infatuation left its traces in other ways. Over the next seventy-five years Joe indulged in occasional bouts of literary and artistic pretension − writing poetry, making sculptures − which sat oddly with her customary no-nonsense bluntness.

More strikingly, she devised her own theatrical games, elaborate practical jokes to startle and mock her friends. And, like Dolly, she came to define herself through a male *alter ego*, a spirit with which she enjoyed an 'almost mystical' relationship more powerful than any of her attachments to the living.

3

~~~~~~~~~~~~~~~~

THE ACTION OF TESTICULAR PULP

While Joe Carstairs was in Paris learning to live like a man, her mother, elsewhere in the city, was pursuing the secret of masculinity in a more concrete form.

In 1917 Evelyn Bostwick, aged forty-four, was appointed laboratory assistant to Serge Voronoff, a French surgeon of Russian extraction, at the Collège de France in Paris. By dint of this she became the first woman admitted to the college.

Voronoff was an unusually tall man, about 6 foot 5 inches, with dark hooded eyes, a thick moustache and a commanding, haughty presence. He was fifty-two in 1918, when he and Evelyn presented to the French Academy of Science a paper describing their experimental treatment of wounds, a project prompted by the casualties of the war. The paper, entitled *Intensive Acceleration of the Healing of Granulating Wounds by the Application of Testicular Pulp*, explained how the pair

35

had 'inflicted 74 wounds on dogs, ewes and goats' and applied to them the living pulp of a variety of glands: the thyroid and adrenal glands, the pancreas, spleen and testicles. Their aim was to test the capacity of these glands to speed up the healing process.

In the published paper Evelyn was pictured holding a goat, its back covered with a sheet from which eight holes had been cut, four on either side of the spine. The caption explained that wounds were made through the holes and each then filled with the pulp of a different gland. Voronoff and Evelyn claimed, impossibly, that their experiments had proved the remarkable healing properties of testicular pulp: 'the action of testicular pulp becomes manifest from its *very first application*, and surpasses all the other glands we have experimented with.' It is not clear whether Evelyn and Voronoff were fraudulent, technically incompetent, or in the grip of a powerful delusion.

These experiments marked the beginning of the couple's obsession with testicles. Serge Voronoff himself had become interested in the subject in 1898, when he saw some eunuchs on a visit to Cairo and pondered on the connection between their castration and their physical debility. These eunuchs, he noted, were often obese, with smooth hairless faces, enlarged breasts and pelves, pendulous cheeks, high-pitched voices and pale skin and gums; what was more, they aged prematurely, were feeble-minded and lacked courage or enterprise.

The eunuchs Voronoff described were grotesque parodies of old women. The twin horrors they represented were the collapse into age and into womanliness. The testicles, he surmised, warded off both evils.

Voronoff did not have the means to pursue his insight until he met Evelyn in 1917. She proved a great supporter of his work, not only as a financial investor but also as a keen participant in his experiments. A recent biographer of Voronoff, David Hamilton, suggests that she may have been too keen: 'It should be noted that Evelyn Bostwick, his assistant, was an ambitious person without laboratory training, and as such she might well have been over-anxious to produce the desired result.' Spurred on by their supposed success in treating wounds with testicle pulp, the couple grafted portions of young ram testicles into the scrotums of old rams. They claimed that these transplants transformed timid, spiritless creatures into bellicose, vital animals with strong sexual drives, thick wool coats and sprightly gaits.

When Voronoff published his results in 1919, he suggested that men too might benefit from testicular grafting. His findings were greeted with great popular curiosity: the possibility of sexual rejuvenation had acquired an added relevance in the wake of the war, when many women had to look to the older generation for husbands. The scientific establishment was more sceptical – Voronoff provided only anecdotal evidence and some inconclusive photographs – but thanks to

Evelyn's money the experiments could proceed without official endorsement. In 1920 Voronoff married Evelyn and performed his first monkey-to-man transplant. (A friend later asked Joe if she thought any of her mother's husbands had married her for her money. 'I think all of them did,' Joe replied.)

A man and an ape were laid on separate tables in an operating theatre, with a surgeon assigned to each. The ape was anaesthetised and shaved, while a local anaesthetic was applied to the man's genitals. One of the ape's testicles was then cut open and sliced into six pieces, and one of the man's opened and scarified with small scalpel cuts. One by one the slices of monkey testicle were carried over to the other table, and stitched separately into the man's scrotum with catgut; the whole was sewn up with silk.

The first two grafts, performed in June 1920, were disastrous. The testicles of both patients had already been destroyed by tuberculosis, and the transplant operations awakened the dormant infections. The grafts had to be rapidly removed. The Voronoffs managed to hush up these failed experiments for a few months. They travelled to America in July, on the death of Nellie Bostwick, and Evelyn skilfully deflected journalists' enquiries about the progress of Voronoff's research. 'I am his mouthpiece,' she told them, 'and anything I say about his work can be taken as coming from him.'

A reporter from the *New York Times* interviewed Evelyn. 'She is rather small and pretty,' he wrote, 'and looked to be in her early thirties, although I learned that she was considerably older. She has reddish-brown hair, worn in simple fashion, and large, intelligent, bluish-gray eyes . . . She was amazingly at home in her subject, and my wonder grew as I noticed her facility of expression and lucidity.' That year, Evelyn's translation into English of Voronoff's *Life: a means of restoring vital energy and prolonging life* was published in New York.

In November Voronoff embarked on a string of gland-grafting operations. He reported spectacular results: his patients, he said, regained their potency and vigour, their mental powers and – in some cases – their hair. He boasted particularly of the astonishing rejuvenation of Edward Liardet, a seventy-four-year-old Englishman who claimed himself transformed by the operation: he had taken up running and weightlifting, and sent Voronoff pictures to prove it. Liardet was an alcoholic, who went on to die of delirium tremens in 1923; it is possible that his apparent transformation was the result of the temporary abstention from tobacco and alcohol that Voronoff required of his patients. Certainly it is scientifically impossible that monkey glands could be accepted by the human body, let alone work the miracles that Voronoff claimed.

Serge Voronoff's experiments were driven by a

conviction that the male genitalia held the secret of rejuvenation, and Evelyn readily subscribed to this doctrine. Joe Carstairs too – despite her loathing for Voronoff – seemed to believe that masculinity and youth were powerfully linked, that by casting off her femininity she might also cast off her mortality. She would try to restore the spent manhood of the Great War in her own person.

Joe Carstairs never discussed her mother's gland-grafting work. She told only two stories about her parents. They were first and final scenes, and both took place in 1918.

Evelyn got wind of her daughter's homosexual affairs, and summoned her to her rooms in Paris. 'She said, "Come and see me," in her lofty way,' recalled Joe, 'and I did. In the Majestic Hotel, if I remember rightly. She wasn't too bad with dope.'

'I know,' said Evelyn. 'I know about you.'

'Really?' asked Joe.

'Yes, you are a lesbian. I've heard all about it. All over Paris.' Joe must buckle down and get married, Evelyn warned, or she would be disinherited.

'Well, I'll tell you,' said Joe. 'I don't like the husband you're married to' – Voronoff – 'and I think the whole thing's a horror. I think he's a murderer. If you want to cut me off, go ahead, I don't give a goddamn about money. Speak your words.'

'If you don't do what I want you to,' replied Evelyn, 'just walk out that door.'

'Thank you, mother,' said Joe, and walked out.

Joe Carstairs added an odd postscript to this tale. She explained that while she lived in France she drove a grey, open Buick, a gift from her mother, and that after their quarrel the car was withdrawn. 'I loved this Buick,' Joe said. 'Of course when I fell short with my mother the Buick left, and I left, and that was it.' In this phrasing, Joe replaces her mother with the Buick: it is the Buick that Joe loves and leaves, the Buick that leaves her. Inanimate objects were wonderful shields against pain.

Since Voronoff and Evelyn did not marry until 1920, Joe's claim that she argued with her mother about her fourth husband in 1918 does not hold up. There are other anomalies in her account of the showdown with Evelyn. The punchline of Joe's story is that she defied her mother, but she seems in the event to have complied – at least nominally – with Evelyn's demands. In 1918, to secure her inheritance, Joe married her childhood friend Count Jacques de Pret.

Joe must have relived the moment of her breakup with her mother often enough to let several quarrels meld. And, characteristically, she told a story in which she walked out on her mother before her mother – in dying – had a chance to leave her.

(Evelyn died aged forty-eight, on March 3 1921, the

day after Voronoff's eleventh monkey-gland operation. She left gambling debts and, said Joe, 'a tremendous debt of cigarettes'. Though Evelyn had probably succumbed to the effects of drugs or drink, her death was ascribed to natural causes. Joe Carstairs believed that Voronoff had killed her mother. 'He was like a vulture,' Joe said. 'A dreadful man. He did murder her, dammit. Got his doctor friends to sign the death certificate. He gave her an overdose. He stood to inherit — it was too easy.' There is no evidence to support this allegation but Evelyn's legacy provided Voronoff with a huge income for the rest of his life. Ten years after her death Voronoff married Gerti Schwartz, a 'cousin' of the mistress of King Carol of Romania; she was believed in fact to be the mistress's daughter by the King. In 1951 Voronoff died, his monkey-gland surgery utterly discredited.)

If Joe did marry Count Jacques de Pret to appease her mother, it was an appeasement laced with spite: Joe believed that he and Evelyn were lovers. Jacques readily agreed to Joe's suggestion that they marry and split the $10,000 dowry. After the wedding they parted immediately and amicably. Even in old age Joe was at pains to point out that the marriage was never consummated. Jacques de Pret, who was known as something of a ladies' man, used his share of the money to foot the bills he ran up on women; Joe went straight out to buy two resplendent uniforms in khaki barathea, a fabric of wool and silk. She recalled these outfits vividly: the collars could be taken off and turned when dirty, and the whole was cleaned by immersion in gasoline. 'I really thought I was something,' Joe said. 'I really thought I was something unbelievable.' The question of quite what she was never seemed to concern Joe: she knew that she was something else, and that delighted her.

The story Joe told about her father went like this: When the war in France ended in November 1918 Joe Carstairs left Paris for London. Perhaps dressed in her new finery, she went to an officers' club in Pall Mall; there, she said, Albert Carstairs was pointed out to her across the bar. She approached him.

'Well, young man?' he asked. 'What do you want?'

'I'm your daughter, sir,' Joe replied.

Colonel Carstairs bought her a drink and gave her a cigar. She told him of her suspicions that her mother had been murdered by Voronoff and he told her, 'Don't touch it. You'll get in trouble.' This was the last time she saw him. Joe was under the impression that he ended his days in India, having contracted a strange disease. (He may have died the next year, since by 1920 his name no longer appeared in the Reserve of Officers list.)

Their brief encounter smacks of fiction – it resembles a scene from a sentimental film, rendered slightly strange by the moment of mistaken sexual identity.

Perhaps the passage of time drained the occasion of its feeling, reduced it to its bare bones and transformed it from drama to ritual. The blurring effects of time might also account for the story's minor inacuracies (Albert Carstairs was not a colonel but a major) and oddities (how did Joe pass for a man in 1918, when all her uniforms had skirts and she had a great mass of hair?). But the story, like the one about Joe's mother, contains an impossibility. Evelyn did not die until 1921, so Joe cannot have discussed her death with Albert Carstairs in 1918. This element at least is fantasy.

But true, half-true or imagined, the story was precious to Joe Carstairs and she recounted it often. Having broken with her mother, she was blessed by her father. It was another would-be deathbed scene, in which Joe's father passed to her his cigar and she, in her splendid new costume, replaced him. Sometimes when she referred to him she made slips to effect this replacement. 'My father was divorced at the age of four,' Joe said, substituting herself for him in mid-sentence. 'My mother was married four times,' she said, 'and I was the first.'

These last meetings were the talismanic scenes by which Carstairs at once remembered and dispensed with her parents.

4

WHAT DO YOU WANT WITH EGGS AND HAM?

With the Great War over, Joe Carstairs looked around for a fresh battlefield. She found one in Ireland, where Sinn Fein was waging a sporadic guerrilla war against the British. Joe enlisted with the Women's Legion Mechanical Transport Section, Dublin, a band of forty young women serving as drivers to British officers.

In Dublin she struck up a firm friendship with Barbara and Molly Coleclough, aged twenty-one and twenty-two, who had joined the Legion soon after its formation two years earlier; they had 'succumbed', in Molly's words, 'to the motor fever and the urge to do one's bit'. Molly and Bardie had been educated at a convent and then a finishing school but both were adventurous, unconventional young women. Bardie in particular was feisty and rebellious; years later, her niece reflected that 'she should have been a boy'. She was nicknamed 'Miss Know-All' by Joe: 'She knew everything, she did everything.'

The girls referred to Joe Carstairs as Tuffy de Pret. 'Our first meeting was typical of her,' Molly wrote in her memoirs. 'She handed me a cigarette case of platinum and gold, which proved to be empty. So we smoked my cigarettes!' Joe was not inclined to hollow pretension or to meanness with money; the 'typical' quality of this gesture lay rather in its combination of swagger and self-deprecation. She loved to show off but she loved also to put others at their ease.

Molly and Bardie put Joe up in their digs. She slept on a campbed and used the other girls' overcoats as blankets. Joe was always running late for roll-call at the barracks, and was often to be seen tearing along the streets of Dublin with her boots unlaced, clutching her breakfast in her hands and finishing the last lap by springing on to a 'jaunting car', or horse-drawn trap. Her long tangle of hair was pulled into a bun, Molly noted, 'like a hedgehog or pin cushion, simply stuffed with pins which stuck out in every direction'. Joe soon got rid of her cumbersome hair, and for the rest of her life wore it in a close crew-cut. A few of the girls in Dublin were already sporting short styles. Bardie had bobbed her hair almost as soon as she joined the Legion, for which she came close to being sacked by the colonel whose car she drove. 'She also', wrote Molly, 'took to wearing men's boots and puttees for some reason which I have never fathomed.'

Joe and the Coleclough sisters were in Ireland during the uneasy lull between two storms – the Easter Rising in 1916 and Bloody Sunday in 1920. In the intervening years anti-British feeling was coming to a boil. The Volunteers, subsequently the IRA, gathered their strength, and secured arms by laying ambushes, raiding police stations and making lightning attacks on patrols. In January 1919 the Volunteers killed two constables and made off with their gelignite; the raid marked the start of the Troubles.

The women drivers' work could be dangerous – the republicans ambushed officers' cars, and pelted them with hot tar – but Joe's recollections were breezy. She spoke only of poker games and high-spirited japes: one night the girls slipped out of their barracks after curfew to steal a Sinn Fein flag. In their free time they took to the hills in a battered old car and visited lakes and country houses. In the barracks they ate from a vending machine – you put sixpence in, and mashed potato and sausage were spewed out. They sang joshing songs about the food: 'What do you want with eggs and ham/When you've got drainpipes in your lamb?'

In early 1919 a dozen of the Dublin girls, including Joe, Molly and Bardie, volunteered to relieve male drivers in northern France. There was much work to be done clearing battlefields, supervising prisoners-of-war, administering hospitals, burying the dead and reconstructing towns. A belt of land 500 miles long was waste as a desert: orchards, forests, canals, farms had vanished and in places the earth itself had to be remade – some hills had lost ten yards in height.

The first batch of women drivers went over on 18 June; by the end of July there were 250 in northern France. Molly and Bardie sailed to Boulogne and went on to a camp at Wimereux. 'An advance party had already arrived,' wrote Molly, 'amongst them de Pret, who had been told she was too young to drive in France. She was happy as a sandboy, helping everyone to mouldy bread, margarine, powdered milk and jam that tasted of paraffin!' Like girl guides embarked on a great adventure, they relished the hardship and camaraderie ahead. Joan Mackern, who became friends with Joe and the Colecloughs in France, recalled in her unpublished memoirs that when she arrived at Wimereux she was boarded in a hotel which had served as a hospital. 'Before our evening meal we all had to get down on our knees and scrub the very dirty floors where there had been large patches of stale blood. The next day we went on to the lovely sands and bathed and basked in the sun.' In 1917 Joan had delivered a dispatch to the Ministry of Munitions during a bombing raid, and was appointed OBE 'for courage and devotion to duty while in grave personal danger'; in the back of her car was a shell-shocked soldier, who shook and cried with fear. It was, she said, the first time she had seen a man weep.

From Wimereux the British drivers were sent to camps at Béthune (where they slept in marquees), at Hersin-Coupigny (where they stayed in log bungalows in the woods), and at Valenciennes (where they were put up in Nissen huts). At the Béthune camp, a former aerodrome, they parked their ambulances in hangars which had housed bomber aircraft. The 'Chinks', as the Chinese labourers in the camps were called, used hot tools to beat out patterns on spent shell cases which they found in the fields, and sold their curious jewels to the English girls. The women too made use of the cast-offs of war: Joe wore an overcoat which had belonged to a friend's brother, a soldier who had been killed.

In their ambulances Joe and her friends drove wounded soldiers from casualty clearing stations to large hospitals. They sold British army huts to the French made homeless by the war. They ferried the Chinese labour battalions and German prisoners-of-war to and from work. And they acted as chauffeurs to officers organising the clearance of ammunition dumps and the reburial of the dead in Imperial War Graves cemeteries – most of the millions of victims had been shallowly buried just beneath the surface of the soil. Wherever they turned the English women saw men dead, crippled, enslaved, so weakened that they depended now on women even to move.

Driving required strength as well as skill. Steering was difficult, the cars' metal frames were heavy, their brakes sluggish; the engines whirred like threshing machines, and a car could tip over if it took a corner too quickly. The roads were sunk with craters, and passed through devastated land – churned-up fields of mud, sunken artillery, blasted trees, barbed wire, shell-holes, dug-outs, trenches. The debris of war was everywhere. The girls drove through the ruins of Ypres, of Lens, of Douai. The driving conditions were so poor that tyres frequently punctured, brakes gave out and springs broke. The women carried out their own repairs.

Joe, Bardie, Molly and Joan chopped wood for their stoves and baths, and in the evenings, dressed in boiler suits and blue berets, worked on their cars in the docks. Joe donned the uniform with gusto, and continued to wear a beret through the 1920s. She did not think twice about adopting a masculine identity: she put on men's clothes for practical reasons, and she kept them on. If anything, Joe delighted in a degree of notoriety. In France she came to be known as 'Klep', because she purloined whatever took her fancy. On one occasion she wrote 'Kleptomaniac' on a hut wall and was reported to the camp supervisor by another girl, who did not know the meaning of the word but assumed it was 'something disgusting'.

Though much of their work was strenuous and grim, the girls also swam in the river, organised picnics, watched the officers' polo-matches, went on clandestine trips to Paris, listened to records, and sat up late playing poker and drinking Balsac. They took the cars out against Army regulations, making runs into the local town for meals. They went also to the patisserie in Arras, the first shop in the ruined city to reopen after the war – 80 per cent of its buildings had been razed. 'Madame would put us in their little room behind the shop to hide us,' wrote Joan Mackern, 'and she would bring us steaming cups of coffee or chocolate and plates of delicious cakes and cherry tarts.' These were golden, liberating days: the old world had been wiped out and the women were building a new world, and new selves, as they pleased.

Joe's private endeavour, her attempt to bury the past and make herself afresh, chimed with the post-war project of burial and reconstruction. The slaughter of the previous four years is barely referred to either in her recollections or the memoirs of her friends. But though they did not mention the carnage, the girls did remember their fear of the Chinese labourers.

One night Molly, Bardie and Joe set out to explore the caverns beneath Arras, against the orders of their commanding officer. During the war 20,000 Allied troops had sheltered in the network of tunnels and caves in the chalky underbelly of the town, while Arras was shelled to pieces above them. The caves were dark, dank, slippery, a maze of passages. 'Our adventure was short-lived,' wrote Molly. 'We got to the bottom and were feeling our way along, when we saw lights showing in the distance and coming towards us, we turned tail and ran hell for leather back up the shaft. When we had nearly reached the top we turned round, to see several "Chinks" at the bottom with torches, staring up at us. We never suggested exploring caverns again, but I do still wonder what nefarious deeds took place in those subterranean passages.'

The women touched upon and recoiled from the Chinks, fascinated and terrified by their 'nefarious deeds'. Like the French fields, the Chinks were pockmarked and scarred, and they seemed to have a dangerous subterranean life. The girls' foray into the shaft was a journey to the underworld, beneath the land and into the graves of the soldiers they were helping to bury.

The Chinese working alongside the girls had, unlike them, been witness to the bloodshed in the French fields. Between 1917 and the beginning of 1918 the British had shipped 100,000 men from Shantung to labour behind the lines, and now the Chinese were assigned to the roughest of the clearing-up work — dismantling barbed wire, filling shell-holes, collecting the remains of dead soldiers. Molly recalled that the girls were 'generally rather scared' of the Chinese labourers. 'They were a motley crew, and all appeared to have had small-pox at some time, poor things . . . They were a funny lot too; it was nothing to see them wearing six or eight hats one on top of the other, all different shapes and colours.' Joan Mackern claimed, rather more brutally, that 'on the whole they were lazy and useless', adding that 'almost a murder took place' when a girl paid one Chinese worker more than another for a decorated bullet case. Molly had a similar experience: 'I remember one said he would knife me because I had ordered an engraved shell case from him, and he had spoiled it by making it black and I refused to have it. One was always hearing tales of them being found murdered.' When a French family refused to open the door to Molly, stranded in the countryside on a freezing night, she surmised that it was due to their fear of 'marauding Chinks'. The Arras archives do record nine Chinese men proceeded against for murder in 1920, but the Chinese labourers in France were hardly 'marauding': they had gained a reputation for great stoicism and industry. If the English women found them ugly and horrifying, it may be because they served as symbols, or repositories, of an ugly and horrifying war.

The girls were demobilised on 23 April 1920. They crossed the Channel and took the train to Victoria, where they were met by charabancs. That night Joe treated the Colecloughs and Joan Mackern to the theatre – they saw the American musical comedy *Irene* at the Empire – and put them all up at the Jermyn Hotel.

Joe paid Bardie Coleclough an income for the rest of her life, and they corresponded regularly. Even when both women were in their eighties Bardie continued to refer to the journey into the caves. 'Klep! Remember our adventure at Arras into the tunnel where we went down . . . and pushed open a door to find a room lighted by flaming torches full of Chink murderers – we turned and ran *fast* up that tunnel . . . We might never have been heard of again.'

They had come home from France hungry for men's work. 'War virilised them,' wrote Colette of her fellow Frenchwomen, 'clothed them with the brief tunic of Eliacin, cropped their hair like the knob of a banister, plastered it down like Argentine dancers.' If the men who had served in the Great War were exhausted and depleted, these women returned replenished, brimming with vigour and ambition.

5

AN UNKNOWN QUANTITY

Joe's grandmother Nellie Bostwick survived five strokes, but on 27 April 1920, four days after Joe was demobilised, she suffered a heart attack and died in New York aged seventy-seven. She was worth some $30 million. Nellie had been Joe's protector and, pending the execution of her will, Joe claimed that she found herself almost penniless. The sudden hardship did not ruffle her: 'I was *supremely* happy,' said Joe, 'I really was.' She took jobs as a bartender in Margate and as a demonstrator at the Bugatti showroom in London. She worked with Molly and Bardie Coleclough at their brother's chicken farm at Hummersea, near Bournemouth, and sold the eggs to the Cunard line at Southampton. Joe lived in a caravan and in cold, gaslit digs from which she drove a motorcycle to work. On occasion she was so hungry that she stole food from shops, living up to her nickname Klep – 'I found that it was necessary,' she said, 'and I didn't consider it wrong.' Joe made her own laws, set her own limits, with a breezy disregard for the rights of others.

In fact, Joe was never short of money. Before her death Nellie had created two trust funds for Joe – the first, in 1918, may have been prompted by Evelyn's rejection of her daughter. Joe's income in 1921 was almost $145,000 and it rose to more than $200,000 the next year. Her poverty was a fantasy, designed to prolong the invigorating privations of the war. To recreate those golden days Joe hatched a plan: she, Molly, Bardie and Joan Mackern would pool their resources, which included stipends from the Army, and set up a chauffeuring business in London.

The X Garage – 'X', Joe explained, to indicate that it was 'an unknown quantity' – was based off Cornwall Gardens, Kensington. The girls lived in a flat above the garage, a converted stable in a cobbled cul-de-sac sunk behind the main square. They bought a handful of six-seater Daimler landaulettes, luxurious cars with staid, sumptuous carriages. The brochure they produced to advertise the business pictured a girl at the wheel of one of the cars, dressed in jacket, cap and tie; over the illustration was a commendation issued at their demobilisation by Sir Ernest Birch KCMG. 'I have always admired in all of you your pluck,' wrote Sir Ernest, 'your enterprise, your hard work, your excellent driving and your cheeriness.'

These women had come back from the first mechanised war with a mastery of machines. 'God knows I'm a damn good driver,' Joe said. The X Garage brochure explained that thanks to their wartime experiences the drivers were familiar with the countryside of Ireland, Great Britain, France and Belgium, and that they spoke French, Italian and German. (Bardie and Molly had presumably acquired their languages in finishing school rather than on the battlefield.) The girls took tourists on expeditions to Imperial War Graves cemeteries in France and Belgium, happily profiting from the memorials to the men who had made way for them. They also offered touring holidays to Ireland, Wales and the Lake District, Devon and Cornwall and the Scottish lochs. The 1,700-mile tour of Ireland took twenty days and cost £134, to cover all expenses for five passengers, including accommodation.

The girls were prepared to take on any driving work, far or near. Bardie and Joan enlisted the hall porters at prestigious London hotels as agents, promising a ten per cent commission on any work put their way. The Savoy proved especially lucrative, and the X Garage cars were frequently booked to pick up parties from the theatre. At four o'clock one afternoon a cable arrived requesting that an American family be met in Naples in less than a week's time; by 5.30 p.m. Bardie Coleclough was on the road in a Daimler. When she reached Naples, Bardie discovered that the Americans' child refused to sit in the car for long periods, so the family travelled between cities by train and Bardie drove ahead to meet them at each stop on their itinerary.

The women delighted in the absurdities and surprises their work threw up. When interviewed by the press they told merry anecdotes about their adventures. One of the girls drove an eccentric American and his secretary on a six-month journey through France, Spain and Morocco to Tunisia. The man announced he would change his collar only when he reached a certain page of his book, and stuck to his guns even when it became apparent that the journey was far too chaotic for sustained reading. The chaos sprang partly from the fact that many of the landmarks picked out in their ancient Baedeker had been destroyed in the war, and partly from the American's complicated superstitions: in the third week of the month, for instance, he insisted on finding a large hotel so that he could book into room 333, while in the fourth week he favoured room 444.

A party of miners from South Wales regularly booked two X Garage cars to take them on their annual trip to the Derby. The miners saved up all year for this treat, for which they hired suits from Moss Bros. A waiter from the Savoy accompanied the group and served a sumptuous lunch of salmon mayonnaise, wine, chicken, strawberries and cream, which the chauffeuses were invited to share.

The X Garage had illustrious clients, among them James Barrie, the author of *Peter Pan*, and the Sultan of Perak. When the Sultan and his unofficial wife visited England, the X Garage girls drove them to all their engagements, including a lunch at St James's Palace with the Prince of Wales. The Sultan gave his drivers silver cigarette cases and placed an order with them for a Minerva car, a present for the Rajah Premaseri. He specified that he wanted it repainted in bright violet, hung with violet satin curtains, and emblazoned on the door with his crest, as big as a dinnerplate, in green and gold. As a final booking, he asked Joan to drive his new polo ponies to Marseilles.

The novelty of female drivers was such that passengers were often confused as to whether to treat their chauffeuses as servants or equals. Sometimes a driver would be shown to the drawing-room when she turned up to collect her charges, sometimes to the kitchen. One driver took a party on a picnic, and was offered no share in the food until a custard tart was blown into the road. The hostess picked up the tart, dusted it off and passed it to the chauffeuse: 'You won't mind this,' she said, 'will you, dear?'

This confusion of status appealed to Joe. She was a woman in the guise of a man, an heiress in the guise of a servant: such ambiguities not only played to her sense of theatre, they were also tools to disconcert and outwit. Behind the wheel of a car, she was at the service of her customers and yet in control of them, literally in the driving seat. And though she and her fellow drivers were to some extent biddable, they also had an independence which the grand ladies they drove about could only dream of. Newspapers pictured the garage girls in oil-stained boiler suits, grinning as they changed tyres and burrowed in engines. They told the press that they had decided to employ no men: 'After employing both men and girls,' said Joan Mackern, 'we have found that the girls are much more adaptable and trustworthy.'

In the early 1920s such remarks were reported in the press with fairly good humour – these women, war workers after all, were admired as spirited modern girls. Because of the war there were almost two million more women than men in Britain and it seemed natural that some of these 'superfluous women', hard-pressed to find husbands, would try their hand at traditionally male jobs. But within a few years the bold new girls bred by the Great War were to excite anxiety and fear.

For herself Joe bought a two-cylinder Triumph, in which she and Bardie sped round Devon and Cornwall; a Sunbeam, in which they took a trip to Sicily; and four silver-grey Rolls-Royces – a flashier, more modern make than a Daimler. In the South of France Joe would get drunk with her half-brother, Frank, with whom she enjoyed a rivalrous camaraderie, and race her Rolls against his. Sixty years later Bardie remembered Joe as she was then, 'sparkling, gay and crazy'.

Cars provided the danger on which Joe thrived. She liked to tell stories of charmed escapes from death. On a rainy night in London in 1921 she and her friends were returning from a party when the driver of their car fell asleep and crashed into a streetlamp outside the Brompton Oratory. Joan, knocked unconscious, vomited on her pale blue evening gown. Molly and Bardie were admitted to hospital with minor injuries and shock. Joe, though badly cut with glass, refused to get into an ambulance and stumbled away bleeding profusely from her limbs and belly. Once home she telephoned her paediatrician, by then a retired doctor of eighty-four, and asked him to come to her aid. 'He came blowing up the stairs,' said Joe, 'and by an electric light in the garage he stitched me up.' He then ordered her to go to a nursing home for two weeks and drink steak blood.

In the early 1920s Joe lived on a secluded estate, at once rugged and luxurious, near the Coleclough farm in Hampshire. Here she converted two disused army huts into a large bungalow which she named Bostwick, after her mother's family. Bostwick foreshadowed the cloistered world she was to create in the Bahamas. In the living-room was a wide window looking out over the sea and the Isle of Wight. Joe had an orchard and fruit walks planted, and a huge rockery laid. She built stables, garages, a tennis court, a croquet lawn, a swimming-pool and guest houses linked by a private telephone system. To service her estate, Joe employed a large staff, including a chauffeur, grooms and seven gardeners.

When Bardie Coleclough brought her nephew and niece on a visit, Joe gave miniature mechanical cars to the boy and dolls to the girl; both children played with a mechanical boat in the pool. Joe too played with boats. Her first was *Sonia*, a magnificent yacht which she referred to admiringly as 'a real terrible girl'. Joe was soon an equally magnificent yachtswoman – she won one race at Harwich despite falling overboard half-way through – and in 1924 *Sonia* took almost every cup in her class.

That year, Joe became even richer. Both Nellie's and Evelyn's wills, which had been subject to three years of litigation, were finally settled. Evelyn's will had been contested by her second and fourth husbands, Francis Francis Sr and Serge Voronoff, and by Joe. Evelyn had left her personal effects to Joe and all the income from the residue of the estate to Voronoff, to pass to Joe on his death. Joe claimed that she was entitled in addition to stock set apart by her mother as a marriage settlement. Francis and Voronoff argued that since Joe's marriage to Jacques de Pret had been annulled in 1921 this settlement was invalid. (Presumably Joe had delayed annulling her marriage until after her mother died, precisely so that Evelyn would not withdraw the settlement.) Francis also insisted that his children, Sally and Francis Jr, were entitled to half the estate. The compromise reached in 1924 was that Joe would receive the marriage settlement, Voronoff would receive his income (about $325,000 a year), and on his death it would be shared between Joe, Sally and Frank. In the same year Joe came into the large fund established for her in Nellie Bostwick's will.

Joe could now afford to marry her two loves — machines and the sea. In 1925 she used her new riches to commission the best motorboat money could buy.

6

~~~~~~~~~~~

THE WATER WHEN ONE HITS IT

Before motor-power, boats had ploughed through the sea, their brute force cleaving a passage by displacing their weight in water. With the invention of the internal combustion engine in the late nineteenth century it became possible to attain much greater speeds by lifting a craft clear of the mass of water, so that it skimmed rather than furrowed. The first successful boats of this type, known as hydroplanes, were introduced in the first years of the twentieth century. Hydroplanes were designed with sharply planed surfaces – or steps – on the bottom of the hull, which at once concentrated the pressure of water on the base, propelling the craft upwards, and sliced the water away from the boat's sides. These long, lean boats were inefficient at low speed but when run fast their hulls climbed to the surface and surfed like pebbles flung across the water.

Hydroplanes were not only faster than conventional

boats but also more dangerous. The water hammered on their flattened bottoms, weakening the wood; when one early hydroplane hit a wave its engine broke clean through the hull and sank. The boats could be capsized by a small swell or the wake of a passing craft. In their flight across a river or lake they could swiftly spin out of control. As these boats became more sophisticated they became more wayward, more mercurial. At a motorboat race in the early 1920s a hydroplane caught in the wash of a tugboat sheered wildly off course and crashed into a stone breakwater, which it then proceeded to climb; at the top of the breakwater it took the leg off a boy who was watching the race. Like the island to which Joe Carstairs was later to devote herself, these new craft were essentially inanimate and yet seemed to contain a vital force, seemed possessed of independent life. Though Joe always referred to boats, cars and the island as 'she', as female entities, she perceived them as virile and wilful. 'I liked the boats,' she said later. 'I liked the way they behaved. I understood them.'

Joe entrusted the design of her hydroplane to Samuel Saunders, the head of the celebrated boat-building firm in East Cowes on the Isle of Wight. In the 1890s Sam Saunders had invented the revolutionary Consuta method of hull-construction, by which moulded wood was backed with oiled fabric and sewn together with copper wire. Saunders built the most successful boat of 1913, the last boat-racing season before the war. The same year his much-loved daughter and assistant, Ethel, died of meningitis aged thirty-four. She was buried in a mahogany coffin of Consuta construction, shaped like a lifeboat, sewn in silver wire and painted white.

Motorboat-racing resumed in 1920 but high-speed boats were so expensive that only a few were commissioned each year, and a successful craft could bring a boatyard great prestige. Joe Carstairs's boat was one of two built by the Saunders yard in 1925. The brilliant young designer Fred Cooper was set to work on it; Sam Saunders supervised the construction.

Joe sat in the Saunders yard in East Cowes to watch the finishing touches to her craft, a seventeen-foot, 1.5-litre or 'Z'-class hydroplane with a shallow hull. The boat's wood was so thin and pliant that it gave when pushed, and bulged in the water with every wave. She was painted gloss black with a single white stripe running her length. To give her extra lift and buoyancy, dozens of inflated pigs' bladders were stowed under the deck. Joe named her *Gwen*, after the Variety star Gwen Farrar, a friend, a lover and an expert horsewoman.

In one of the test runs the boat capsized, and when she came up again Joe renamed her by reversing the letters of her name. Now she was *Newg*. By undergoing this ducking and rechristening the boat became a sister to Carstairs. The boat shared in her own renaming, just as Joe, on regaining consciousness after the fall from the camel in London Zoo, took a new name and became a different creature, inverted and strengthened.

Once the boat was launched Sam Saunders offered Joe Carstairs the services of his own chauffeur and mechanic, Joe Harris. The two Joes became devoted to one another, and Harris rode with Carstairs as her mechanic in almost all her races over the next five years. 'My man was Joe Harris,' was how she put it. She was already known as Joe by the time they met, and she enjoyed the match of names, producing race souvenirs inscribed: '"Joe" and Joe'. The origin of her nickname is obscure but it is interesting that her father's name – of which she claimed to have no knowledge – was Albert Joseph Carstairs.

Joe Carstairs was ready to point out that Joe Harris faced more danger than she during a race: when a motorboat crashed, the mechanic was hurled into the engine behind which he sat, while the pilot was buffered by the wheel. Both Joes were dark, small and stocky. Joe Harris, the shorter of the two, was altogether more crumpled and loose; his face was worn, his jackets were creased, his mouth turned down at the corners and his sweaters rucked in folds across his belly. Carstairs, like a well-fed schoolboy, had a full, smooth face, pressed jackets, regular features, and hair slicked firmly back on to her head. For the camera, she frowned a little, squared her shoulders, held a cigarette in one hand and placed the other in a jacket pocket. Joe Harris looked easy and baggy in his manhood; Joe Carstairs strained after hers. An apprentice mechanic in the Saunders yard recalled how greatly Carstairs cared for Joe Harris, and remarked that he was maybe like a father to her. She was proud of him, certainly. In one picture of the two together she stands ramrod-straight and links his arm possessively as he leans comfortably into her.

Harris was among the first of the scores of people Carstairs 'looked after'. She provided him with an income in perpetuity; when he lost both legs in old age she travelled to England to be at his bedside; and when he died she continued to support his family. 'Joe Harris, my mechanic, was always with me,' she recalled in the 1990s. 'A grand guy. He never accepted a job with anyone else. A very brave chap and a damned good mechanic.'

Newg won her first race on Southampton Water, and was then entered for a series of competitions at Cannes. Joe Carstairs drove down to Cannes from Paris through pelting rain in a Vauxhall capable of 120mph. She arrived in 'a blue funk' after seventeen-and-a-half hours, and though she and Joe Harris took *Newg* to victory in a 20 km race they capsized in the next contest. Hydroplanes were more volatile in the

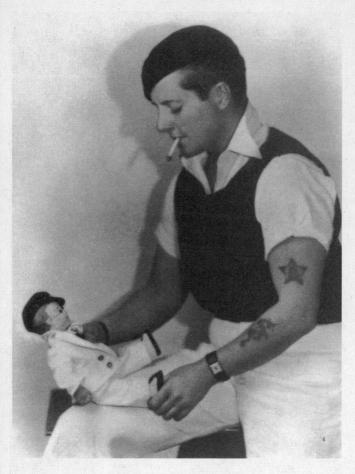

Joe Carstairs with Lord Tod Wadley, late 1920s

'Tuffy, 1905': Marion Carstairs aged five

Evelyn Bostwick, mother of
Marion Carstairs

Thought to be Albert
Carstairs, father

Nellie Bostwick, maternal
grandmother

Joe Carstairs (standing, left) with other members of the Women's Legion, Dublin, 1918

Joe with Ruth Baldwin (left) and another friend on board *Sonia*, early 1920s

Molly Coleclough, Bardie Coleclough and Joan Mackern with an X Garage car, circa 1922

Joe Carstairs in *Newg*, circa 1926

Gar Wood, Joe Carstairs, Joe Harris and another
member of her crew, late 1920s

Joe Carstairs racing *Estelle II* at Detroit, 1928

Mabs Jenkins and Joe after a successful day's
hunting in India, 1931

Ruth Baldwin

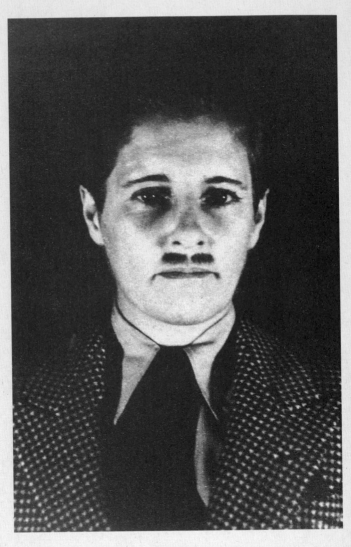

Joe Carstairs wearing a moustache

sea than in rivers. They progressed by a series of jumps and even in small waves might sheer wildly, taking on gallons of water. Each time the hydroplane leapt into the air the throttle had to be closed, to prevent the engine racing and smashing the propeller shaft. If flotsam and jetsam broke open the delicate hulls, the boat could nose-dive to the seabed.

'If you run into a head sea,' Joe told a reporter for the *Evening News*, 'you get a jar absolutely right through you. I can't describe it; there's nothing with which to compare it. It's far worse than any electric shock.' But she played down the danger, insisting that the discomfort of motorboating was much greater. 'Why, at the end of a race you're filthy,' Joe said. 'Spattered with oil, soaked through, and can't hear a thing.'

Joe said that she chose motorboats over other racing machines because 'you get a better idea of speed than in a car or anything else'. The *Birmingham Post* described motorboating as '*par excellence* the sport for the speed enthusiast' — an aeroplane's propellers, by contrast, 'beating against the unresisting air . . . give one hardly any sensation of speed'. Racing a motorboat was a felt battle, a collision between sea and machine, and racers could be knocked unconscious if they were thrown into the water at speed. 'The water when one hits it', said Joe, 'is as hard as a marble floor.' In her boat, Carstairs could live even harder and faster than she did on land.

In June, Joe Carstairs took part in the trials for the second ever Duke of York's Trophy, already acknowledged as the leading motorboating event in Britain. The race had been instituted the previous year in an attempt to standardise the competition between boats, and all entrants were seventeen-foot, one-and-a-half-litre hydroplanes, known as 'mosquitoes' for the manner in which they buzzed across the water. The course consisted of four seven-and-a-half-mile laps of the Thames between Putney and Mortlake. The greatest danger in the race lay in rounding the buoys, where a misjudgement could result in driver and mechanic being thrown out of their craft and into the path of a rival boat.

The newspapers noted Joe's arrival on the motorboating scene with wary, gently mocking admiration. 'A new type of river girl made her appearance on Thames-side on Saturday,' reported one. 'Keen-eyed and close-shingled, with a costume approaching a man's flannel lounge-suit, she stood, on the Surrey bank between Mortlake and Putney talking glibly of outboards, revolutions and baskets.' Remarkably little was made of the novelty of a woman competing in the event, perhaps because no one knew what to make of Joe. Female competitors were so rare that no women's races existed, and she always competed in an all-male field.

In the 1925 contest Joe Carstairs achieved the

fastest time, 32.16 knots, in the second of four rounds ('32 Knots in the Thames,' ran the *Daily Telegraph* headline). But she lost her advantage in the next lap when weeds – a hazard of river-racing – got caught in *Newg*'s propeller. She was placed fifth. The trophy went to Captain Woolf Barnato in *Ardendrun II*.

Woolf Barnato, a diamond merchant and former heavyweight boxer, was one of the most charismatic figures in motorboating. He and Joe became great friends. 'Babe' Barnato's romances with starlets of the London stage were much reported in glossy magazines. Joe, too, enjoyed dalliances with showgirls and actresses, though these of course were not reported in the press.

The joint winner of the previous year's race, John Edward de Johnston-Noad, recalled meeting Joe at the 1925 Duke of York's. Tall, dark-skinned, with a rakish moustache and a Gallic nose, Johnston-Noad always wore a monocle, often a beret and occasionally a tasselled woollen hat. He styled himself Count of Montenegro. Johnston-Noad took to Joe. She was a 'small, dumpy twenty-four-year-old tom-boy', he observed, 'who wore short, clipped hair and dressed like a man . . . The actress Gwen Farrar was only one of [her] many lady friends. I shall always remember Carstairs' tough-faced secretary 'Fatty' Baldwin – otherwise known as Ruth – cheerleading an ever-changing bevy of attractive girl supporters – each of them smartly dressed and given their own motor car.' This last observation may be slightly exaggerated: nowhere else is it claimed that Joe had a fleet of girlfriends with motor cars. But she was certainly generous, and may well have given cars – as emblems of herself, and as vehicles of independence – to some of her friends.

Johnston-Noad had the honour of piloting the Duke of York, the future George VI, around the Thames while the other contenders were warming up for the trials in 1925. The Duke asked to be introduced to the river girl. As they approached Joe Carstairs' craft, which had temporarily halted, she wheeled round furiously, alarmed that she might be disqualified if anyone came to her aid. 'Fuck off! Fuck off!' she shouted. 'Don't you bloody well come near me!' The Duke turned to Johnston-Noad in bewilderment. 'W-w-what's wrong with her, Mr Johnston-Noad?' 'Er, ignition trouble, I believe, Your Royal Highness,' he replied. 'She's changing her plugs.'

Johnston-Noad was born, like Joe, in 1900, and his career as a motorboat racer had been preceded by a childhood even more peculiar than hers. His life serves as a counterpoint to Joe's: their family histories were similar, so was their behaviour in the 1920s; but after the motorboating days they took very different courses. Johnston-Noad was the man Joe could have been but – thankfully – wasn't.

'I was rebellious from the day that I was born,' Johnny Johnston-Noad wrote in his unpublished memoirs, 'nobody wanted me.' Like Carstairs, he blurred cause and effect: he was not rebellious because he was rejected, he suggested, but rejected because he was rebellious.

Johnston-Noad's memoirs are so bizarre that parts of them are difficult to credit. He, like Joe, made a myth of himself. He claimed that his mother, the daughter of the King of Montenegro, was murdered immediately after his birth. His father, he explained, was a Scottish engineer who had made millions in the nitrate mines of Chile and then dabbled in the political intrigues of the mountainous Serbo-Croat state of Montenegro. The King ennobled him in gratitude for his support and allowed him to marry his daughter. But enemies of the Crown killed the princess moments after she delivered her son. Johnston-Noad was not sure that his father, who he believed had connections with the terrorist group the Black Hand Gang, was not himself the murderer.

The boy was brought up by nannies in Paris and Nice; he complained that he was dressed, in the fashion of the day, as a little girl. His father took as his second wife a French countess who loathed her stepson – she made a wax effigy of him, claimed Johnston-Noad, into which she stuck pins – and soon Johnny was despatched to England as a ward of court.

On the crossing a stranger pushed him overboard. He was rescued, but throughout his childhood lived in fear of being murdered by Montenegrans. When it seemed he was being watched he moved from one set of guardians to another, and eventually he changed his name from Howard-Johnston to Johnston-Noad to confuse his enemies.

At first he was cold and miserable in England, and didn't bother to eat. 'Then I joined the Scouts and became a choirboy,' he recalled, 'and that sort of pulled me together. Then I went out fornicating – that helped me a bit more!' His father was killed in a mining disaster in South America in 1919; Johnny claimed he had met him only twice.

Johnston-Noad began racing boats in 1921. He also took up flying and raced cars, on and off the track – the walls of his house were hung at one point with fifty-two summonses for speeding. Like Joe, he was as wild and free in his sexual life as he was on the road and on the sea. In his recollections, motor cars and sex were closely related. 'I have treated every car as a mistress,' he said. The cars were symbols and instruments of sexual freedom. Johnston-Noad owned several Bentleys and designed his own Rolls-Royce with a 'fornication seat' in the back. And though he was married – his wife raced in the minor motorboat contests – he had scores of affairs. When Johnston-Noad's girlfriends came to watch him race, he said, they wore underwear in his colours, black and blue. He described the world he moved in as a 'sporting society . . . sporting in action with cars and boats and sporting in their attitude to life. Everyone was mad. It was a case in those days of not caring and a lot of excessive courage.'

The stories Johnny Johnston-Noad and Joe Carstairs told about their childhoods had much in common: the money mined from metal and oil, the wicked step-parent, the murdered mother, the fleeting father. They both raced away from these unhappy scenes, and countered their abandonment with rebellion – in cars, in boats, in bed.

At the end of the 1920s, though, their stories diverged. Johnston-Noad's unstable nature led him to trouble in the less tolerant 1930s, and into a seedier world. After being bankrupted in the 1929 stock market crash he perpetrated a series of financial scams and was imprisoned in a French jail and three English prisons. By 1952 not even Johnston-Noad's defence lawyer could find much to recommend his client: in court he described him as 'an egotistical megalomaniac who saw life through the romantic spectacles of the hero of a cheap novelette'. Johnny Johnston-Noad was convicted of involvement in a jewel heist master-minded by his second wife, the master-criminal 'The Black Orchid'; she and her lover killed themselves in a suicide pact while on the run from the police.

Johnston-Noad was acquitted, though, of firing two pistol-shots at his mistress during one of his 'bottle parties' and of running a brothel in New Bond Street. And his neighbours near Egham, Surrey, failed to curtail the frolics at his riverside house Fornication Cottage in the late 1930s; they objected in particular to the occasions on which Johnston-Noad and his friends would chase a naked fat woman around the lawn, smacking her on the bottom with paddles.

7

HULLO! MY DEAR FELLOW

At the end of 1925 Joe Carstairs underwent her definitive rebirth. She and Ruth Baldwin – the 'tough-faced secretary' Johnston-Noad had observed – took a skiing holiday to Rosegg, in the Swiss Alps, and on Christmas Day Ruth gave Joe a man-doll. Carstairs traded her life for his.

The doll, a stuffed leather manikin just over a foot high, was manufactured in Germany by the celebrated toymakers Steiff. His limbs were firm and jointed at the body, so the arms and legs could be turned this way and that in alert and expressive poses. His head was round, a neat ear on either side. His eyes were black beads, like shining currants, set wide in innocence and topped with short, lightly arched eyebrows. The soft leather flesh of the face was contoured – the cheeks, the forehead and the chin lifted gently, the nose rose like a button. Beneath the nose, turning up as if to cup it, was a small dark smile, the smile a child would draw, snugly stitched into the leather.

As the doll grew older, his face was to blacken, crack and peel; the stitches binding his head together like a football became dirty and tough, forming the mark of a cross across his face. But his eyes still shone and his smile stuck fast. Joe Carstairs dressed her doll in suits and uniforms. He was a homunculus, a tiny man with the face of a boy. Joe called him Lord Tod Wadley, as if he were a waddling toddler and a peer of the realm together. He was as pure as a lamb, as worldly as a rake, as omniscient as a god.

Ruth Baldwin was the girlfriend Joe loved above all others. Yet there is little trace of her now. Like Dolly Wilde – and like Joe herself in many ways – Ruth performed for the day rather than produced for posterity. Her photographs show what she looked like: tall, long-legged, wide in the shoulders, with a big moon face, bold, naughty eyes and thick auburn hair. Her tombstone tells when she was born (17 February 1905), her full name (Catherine Ruth Baldwin) and the date of her death (31 August 1937). Her nicknames were Bobby and – according to Johnston-Noad at any rate – Fatty. She was said to be of Irish stock, like Dolly Wilde, and American by birth. When Joe died, there was one man still alive who had known Ruth, but he was too old and ill to want to talk about her; friends said he had been responsible in the 1930s for fetching her home from bars. All of Joe's friends had heard of Ruth: 'She was wild,' they said. 'She was such fun. Ruth, she was really *wild*.' The stories they passed on about her were, like Ruth, brief and bright.

Ruth took drugs. She drank – she replaced her kitchen with a bar. She was, according to Joe, 'fabulously strong'. She was promiscuous and possessive. She freely spent Joe's money. She ate raw chops in the middle of the night. She liked to take her pet Pekinese to the pub and feed him brandy. She taught Joe that: 'The world is one's oyster if taken at will.' She was a heady, stormy woman, and it seems that her public wildness was matched by a private wilderness.

Through her association with Dolly Wilde, Joe had brushed shoulders during the war with the lesbian literary circle in Paris. Dolly was still living in Paris in the 1920s, and among the women also attending Natalie Barney's salons was the writer Djuna Barnes. Until 1927, Djuna Barnes lived with a woman named Thelma Wood, and in 1936 she fictionalised their affair in the odd novel *Nightwood*. The ménage Barnes describes is in some respects similar to that of Joe Carstairs, Ruth Baldwin and Lord Tod Wadley.

In *Nightwood*, the narrator reflects on the significance of the doll given to her by her girlfriend, Robin. 'When a woman gives [a doll] to a woman,' she writes, 'it's the life they cannot have, it is their child, sacred and profane . . . Sometimes, if [Robin] got tight by evening, I would find her standing in the middle of the room, in boy's clothes, rocking from foot to foot, holding the doll she had given us – "our child" – high above her head, as if she would cast it down, a look of fury on her face. And one time, about three in the morning when she came in, she was angry because for once I had not been there all the time, waiting. She picked up the doll and hurled it to the floor and put her foot on it, crushing her heel into it: and then, as I came crying behind her, she kicked it, its china head all in dust, its skirt shivering and stiff, whirling over and over across the floor, its blue bow now under now over.' The fiction was based in fact: after parting from Thelma Wood in 1927, Djuna Barnes kept their broken doll by her until she died. (Dolly Wilde herself appears as a kind of doll broken by rage in another of Djuna Barnes's works, *Ladies Almanack* (1928), a parody of Parisian salon society: Barnes casts Dolly as the drug-addicted lesbian Doll Furious.)

Carstairs's family, too, comprised two women and a doll. Joe, like the narrator of *Nightwood*, was the keeper of the doll. Ruth, like the narrator's lover, was drunk, reckless, raging. Although Joe never said that Ruth damaged Wadley, she did in later years express a terror of her girlfriends trying to hurt him. And like the doll in *Nightwood* Wadley was a mock-child, a sacred and profane earnest of the two women's love. Yet unlike the *Nightwood* doll, he was not a fragile substitute for a real child: he was infinitely better. Lord Tod Wadley was not made of china but of leather – his flesh was tougher than human skin. Wadley was a boast rather than an apology. He was the stuff of defiance and comedy.

Joe Carstairs could not bear the idea of having a child. 'I'd never have a baby for anything in the world.' A girlfriend once suggested adoption and Joe ran from the room virtually screaming with horror. It is easy enough to take her at her word – after all, girls were so disturbing to her that she scarcely acknowledged their existence, and the role of the perpetual boy was her own. A real boy-child would first have usurped her and then – in growing to adulthood – undone her dream that boyhood could last for ever. The boy Wadley, though, could be her companion and her model in perpetuity. And her belief in him was itself living proof of her childlike spirit.

In *Nightwood* too, the doll is not just the child two women cannot have but the child they long to be. Djuna Barnes depicts homosexuality as a transcendent immaturity, embodied in the doll: 'The last doll . . . is the girl who should have been a boy, and the boy who should have been a girl! . . . The doll and the immature have something right about them, the doll because it resembles but does not contain life, and the third sex because it contains life but resembles the doll.'

Joe and Ruth lived together at a house Joe bought

for £3,000 in Mulberry Walk, off the King's Road in Chelsea. The house had thick brick walls covered in grapes and inset with little windows like portholes on to the street, while inside it was bright with skylights. It was at once as spacious and enclosed as an ocean liner. There were huge living-rooms and bedrooms equipped with bunks – Joe lived upstairs, Ruth down. Joe's floors were laid with battleship linoleum. A charwoman – 'old fat Mrs Peacock'—did the cooking and a maid lived in a room off the stairs between Joe's apartment and Ruth's.

Behind the house was a small, walled garden with a pond. A few penguins shuffled around the garden for a while; these were eventually donated to London Zoo on account of their unpleasant smell. From then on, Joe was given toy penguins as presents, a practice which persisted until the end of her life: china penguins, feathered penguins, plastic penguins, wooden penguins, furry penguins, marble penguins. The signs of mortality and decay were repulsive to her. 'I prefer inanimate objects,' she said.

By the front door of 5 Mulberry Walk, Joe mounted a plaque which read: 'Marion Barbara Carstairs and Lord Tod Wadley'. The plaque played with the idea that it might be more acceptable that Miss Carstairs be partnered by a fictional aristocrat than a live girl. Tradesmen, Joe said, occasionally called asking for Lord Tod, and once a man turned up at the door claiming to have served with Wadley in France during the Great War.

Many of the growing band of motorboat, car and aircraft racers carried mascots with them for luck. Sometimes Carstairs referred to Wadley as her mascot, but he was far too precious to take out on the water. While she took risks with herself, she would take none with him. Nevertheless, Wadley worked like a charm. In his first year, Joe triumphed in *Newg*.

Tens of thousands of people lined the Thames to watch the 1926 Duke of York's Trophy, which had attracted the strongest international gathering of any race since the war: three British boats (including *Newg* and Johnston-Noad's *Miss Betty*), two from America, two from France, one from Canada and one from Germany. 'Babe' Barnato had supplied a supercharged engine for *Newg*, and he piloted her in the first round; then Joe took over. In the early stages of the race nearly all the hydroplanes packed up, with problems ranging from driftwood damage to ignition failure, and by the final heat only two remained – *Newg*, piloted by Joe, and *Sigrid IV*, piloted by Herr Krueger. In the closing moments the German boat too fell by the wayside, its connecting rod having broken. Then *Newg*'s propeller was caught by a submerged rope. It seemed no one was going to complete the course. But Joe managed to cut the rope free and win the race. 'Shingled Girl Beats German' ran the *Daily Mail* headline the next day.

That season Joe won the Royal Motor Yacht Club International Race, the *Daily Telegraph* Cup, the Bestise Cup and the Lucina Cup. On Lake Windermere she secured the one-and-a-half-litre-class world record — 54.97mph. She commissioned a further one-and-a-half-litre boat from Sam Saunders which, in gratitude, she dubbed *Leumas*, the letters of his name in reverse.

Joe was the most celebrated female motorboat racer in Britain, as fast and as brave as any man. She was thrilled by the attention her victories brought. 'I loved an audience,' she recalled. 'I loved people to come up and say, "Give me your autograph." I was a nasty little piece. With an audience, it's amazing what I can do.'

Wadley provided a perpetual audience for Joe's exploits, as she did for his. He was the archetypal Bright Young Thing. His suits were tailored, like Joe's, in Savile Row, his leather shoes imported from Italy; he had a sealskin coat trimmed with fur. In 1929 a friend dummied up a magazine feature in which Wadley was pictured yachting, riding, taking cocktails, writing a novel and sitting for a studio portrait. In one photograph he is depicted reclining among foliage, spectacles perched on the top of his head, empty bottles strewn about him and an open book lying by his side. Beneath runs the caption: 'I am a thorough student, and when

I feel I must have solitude, I take a day in the country – with my books.' Another caption reads: '"Hullo! My dear fellow": Lord Tod Wadley greets a friend.'

'Like other members of the Bright Young Set,' explains the text, 'he is an all-round sportsman and yachtsman; he also rides and motors. He understands the charm of a really good cocktail, and realises that one cannot be a Success in Society these days without some literary achievement. It is an open secret that he is writing a novel – and that when the book finally appears it will create a sensation by its outspoken analysis of modern Society.' (Olivia Wyndham, who took the pictures for this dummy magazine page, later moved to New York, where she lived with a black woman in Harlem.)

Wadley is not the only doll to feature in photographs from the 1920s – there are snapshots of Joe Carstairs and her friends in Cannes, in Hampshire, in Switzerland holding dolls aloft, perching them on walls, sitting with them among the rocks. Joe did not keep or remember any of these dolls; nor did she ever mention the dolls of her childhood. As a little girl she must have had girl-dolls – elaborate, decorated creatures, with china faces, stiff bodies and lacy layers of clothing. But Joe's desire for a boy-doll – perhaps for the sailorboys and soldiers with which her baby brother played – overcame the memory of all but Wadley.

In the 1920s there was another sailor doll, with a

face bigger and cuter than Wadley's – a more crudely sentimental figure. Joe posed with this doll for press photographs, one of which was reproduced in the late 1980s in a boating magazine. Joe Carstairs, aged eighty-eight, wrote to the author of the article: 'Lord Tod Wadley has been with me for sixty-three years and is actually that age. The picture in the magazine is *not* Lord Tod and I don't know who it is!!' Maybe the rogue Wadley, which Joe could not remember, was a sometime mascot – since she would not endanger the real Wadley by taking him racing with her, she might have taken the mock-Wadley in his place. Wadley was given masks and *alter egos* to protect him too.

In her insistence that Lord Tod Wadley is 'actually that age', Joe effectively dated his birth not from the moment of his manufacture in the toy factory but at the moment he became hers. 'LORD TODD WADLEY is now sixty-two years old for real,' she wrote in another letter in the 1980s. The suggestion is that, like her, Wadley experienced a second, authentic birth when the two of them were joined. Joe's belief in her doll often seems a little crazy, it verges on madness. But, more to the point, it staved off madness. Wadley was the means by which she could split herself in two and – through her bond with him – still be held together.

One night in the mid-1920s after getting drunk ('awfully scratched', as she would describe it), Joe had her arms tattooed. She then sat with Wadley for a photographic portrait: she held him on her knee and gazed thoughtfully down, her muscles bulging with inky stars and dragons, a cigarette in her mouth and a beret at an angle on her tightly cropped hair; he looked back, clean-faced and trusting, in a white sailing suit and a cap cocked to echo hers. In another portrait Joe posed in a sailor's cap and suit, effectively impersonating Wadley, with a woman standing next to her as a foil for her masculinity. She and Wadley were continually changing places, mimicking and recalling each other. Yet another studio portrait of the time shows Wadley alone with his reflection in a mirror. Joe labelled it 'Narcissus'.

8

~~~~~~~~~~~~~~

I DID LOOK LIKE A BOY,
I REALLY DID

The 1920s was an era which instantly mythologised itself, and Joe Carstairs made herself in its image. For a moment she and the world intersected. Joe loved everything the children of the 1920s loved: speed, machines, fancy-dress parties, treasure hunts, cabaret, nightclubs, cocktails, dancing, motor cars, sex, and – above all – boyishness. Joe Carstairs adapted to her era but outdid it, succumbed to the passions of her time and exceeded them. She took 1920s London as her stage; masculine garb as her costume; cigarettes, motor cars, boats and dolls as her props.

Joe was infatuated by the theatre and had affairs with several actresses. The stage was a place of giddiness and licence, where women and men swapped guises as a matter of course. In June 1920, a few weeks after Joe was demobilised, the legendary male impersonator Vesta Tilley gave her last performance on the London stage. 'Vesta Tilley was ever a boy whom nothing could unman,' wrote the critic James Agate. 'Master of her characters, she was mistress of herself.' Another critic, W. R. Titterton, remarked: 'Her soul is the soul of a boy – or perhaps, shall I say, of a girl, at the age when girls and boys are very much alike. She is and always will be a naïve child.' By dressing as a man, it seemed, a woman could elude the constraints both of gender and of age. As she slipped on her costume she slipped off her maturity, and the public saw her not as sexually double but as unsexed. It was a strange kind of vanishing trick. And one particularly suited to an era which made a fetish of both masculinity and youth.

Real boys, after all, were in short supply – so many had died on the battlefields of Europe and many of those that returned were wounded, mutilated or shell-shocked. Women, having had to take up their work during the war, now took up their image. 'Healthy young girls are more boyish than boys,' ran a *Daily Mail* headline in 1921.

From the early 1920s women's fashion became increasingly androgynous. The waistlines on dresses dropped dramatically, erasing the female bust, waist and hips in one fell swoop. Sleeves and skirts short-ened, revealing long stretches of arm and leg, the lither the better. Women wound wide ribbon around their chests to flatten the outline of their breasts. They cut their hair to a bob, then a shingle (as short as a man's on the nape of the neck) and then – though this was considered daring – to an Eton Crop, indistinguishable from a male haircut. Men's clothing was adapted for women: navy-blue blazers, ties, cufflinks, dinner jackets. A few women – Joe included – began to wear Oxford Bags, with billowing trouser-legs that removed any hint of the female form.

A barber came regularly to the house in Mulberry Walk to crop Joe's hair. Her suits and jackets were flawlessly cut by the best tailors, and kept immaculately clean. She wore stiffly starched Peter Pan collars, navy-blue berets, reefer jackets. But she did not consider herself butch: boyishness lent her lightness and elegance. 'I did look like a boy,' Joe said later. 'I really did. But I was not a stomper.'

In his memoirs, Quentin Crisp recalled the fashion of the 1920s: 'The short skirts, bobbed hair, and flat chests . . . were in fact symbols of immaturity . . . The word "boyish" was used to describe the girls of that era. This epithet they accepted graciously.' In pursuit of an athletic slenderness, the young women of the 1920s went on diets, skied, played squash and tennis, raced boats, cars and planes, and trained in the gymnasium. 'Women's fondness for sport fixes the present severe contour,' remarked the fashion designer Monsieur Worth. 'These masculine lines make women look young.' Joe was, and remained, 'absolutely mad on physical fitness'. 'God gave me a marvellous body,' she explained, 'and I like to keep it that way.' Distinctly chubby in 1921, she exercised rigorously to become lean and muscular.

In the 1920s an enthusiasm for sport and for the wholesome pleasures of the great outdoors ran alongside the decadence of the metropolitan scene, its 'dope parties', exotic cocktails and lurid make-up. Joe straddled both worlds. With the Coleclough sisters, she went skiing and tobogganing in Switzerland, rode horses in Hampshire, sailed and swam off the coast. With Ruth and her actress friends, she dressed up and drank and danced through the night. In the countryside Joe sought to preserve and enhance her youth, in London to show it off, to thumb her nose at age. 'I couldn't stand old people,' she said.

Friends noted that Joe had the voice of a professional actress, resonant, full-bodied and with an American lilt. She was theatrical in her behaviour, too. Joe would walk into a room, head straight for the mirror and strike a pose, three fingers inside her jacket pocket, the thumb and little finger outside. 'Marvellous,' she exclaimed. The smouldering expressions of Rudolf Valentino, the idol of the silent screen in the early 1920s, are echoed in several studio portraits of Joe Carstairs. In almost every photograph taken of her at the time, Joe is holding a cigarette. She admitted that though she smoked cigars, cigarettes, cheroots and pipes, it was merely for effect: she never inhaled.

The cigarettes were props, symbols of glamour and masculinity, like the cigars she said she had accepted from her father and Roger de Perigny, and stolen from Francis Francis.

The Canadian actress Beatrice Lillie, a friend of Joe's, became the most celebrated of the male impersonators on the West End stage. 'I was known, in fact,' she recalled in her memoirs, 'as the best-dressed man in London.' Lillie was one of the stars of the *Midnight Follies* floor show at the Hotel Metropole, which ran nightly from 1922. The dining-tables at the Metropole formed a horseshoe around a large dance-floor hung with glowing Chinese lanterns. On the stroke of midnight, three loud knocks signalled the start of the show; the orchestra paused and the diners hurried from the dance-floor back to their tables. Then the performers, many of them having just taken their curtain calls at the theatres of Shaftesbury Avenue and the Strand, emerged from a curtained recess to stage a fast succession of turns – dances, jazz numbers, topical sketches, songs and comic monologues.

In 1925 Gwen Farrar and Norah Blaney appeared at the Metropole. Gwen, an elegant woman with a sleek dark bob and horn-rimmed spectacles, was the woman after whom *Newg* was named. She sang baritone and played piano and cello. Gwen and Norah had met while performing in Army camp concerts during the First World War, and appeared as a double act in

London and provincial variety theatres throughout the 1920s. In 1921 a critic noted that they contributed to 'the musical excellence and the gay repartee' of the revue *Pot Luck* at the Vaudeville. In *The Punch Bowl*, a revue playing at the Duke of York's in 1924, Norah Blaney dressed up as an eighteenth-century Venetian courtier to sing a sentimental ballad; then delivered a comic speech on the removal of the Eros statue from Piccadilly Circus; and then sang with Gwen at the piano. Their partnership was broken off, according to Gwen Farrar's entry in *Who's Who in the Theatre*, in May 1924 and resumed in September 1925 – it may be significant that it was during this interval that Joe named *Newg* for Gwen.

Joe took particular pleasure in beating actresses at their own game, outwitting them with her own disguises and impersonations. On one occasion she called at Norah Blaney's flat dressed as an electrician, in a wig and overalls; she had examined all the light fittings before she was recognised. In a similar costume she put up a ladder outside the house of Gwen Farrar, and plastered the front with posters described by the *Daily News* as 'very inappropriate'.

The theatre had come to the restaurant, the dance-hall and nightclub – and, as if in reply, private parties became exercises in theatre. Fancy-dress parties proliferated in London and dancing became a mania. In 1925 the *Evening News* reported, rather pointedly, that Joe

Carstairs 'can dance a Charleston which few people can partner'. Joe and Ruth threw parties in nightclubs, aboard the *Sonia*, on pleasure boats on the Thames; their parties at Mulberry Walk were so riotous that neighbours petitioned to have the women evicted. At some of these gatherings all the guests ended up in the nude, but the dress code was usually fancy dress – once, as a slightly cruel joke, Joe indicated fancy dress on only half of the invitations. Guests were invited to come to Joe and Ruth's United States party as 'Hijackers, Yegs, Wops, Kikes, Co-Eds, Kappa Kappa Gammas, Arnchies, Buckras, Dictys, Crapshooters, Bums, Gobs, Dames and Pullman Porters'. Joe went as a Marine; Ruth as a Mexican bandit.

In Virginia Woolf's *Orlando*, published in 1928, the hero is a sexual chameleon, who puts on trousers to become a man, skirts to become a woman; clothes, in this fantasy, do not disguise but transform the fluid creature within. 'There is much to support the view that it is clothes that wear us and not we them,' writes Woolf. '[They] mould our hearts, our brains, our tongues to their liking.' The shape-changing parties of the 1920s perfectly suited the half-secretive, half-flamboyant lesbian *demi-monde*. These disguises were at once deceptions and proclamations.

For monied women in the post-war years, it was possible to move in circles where promiscuity was chic, homosexuality new and daring. Though Joe lived with Ruth Baldwin through the late 1920s, she made it a point of honour always to have several girlfriends on the go. Ruth, too, had numerous affairs with others. Their passion for one another seems to have survived intact.

The luminary of the bisexual actresses whom Joe numbered among her friends was Tallulah Bankhead. Having enjoyed moderate success on the American stage, Tallulah took England by storm in 1923, when she was twenty-one. She became a darling of London society, relished for her brazen wit, filthy language and shameless sexual behaviour. 'I'm as pure as the driven slush,' she boasted. Tallulah was a cult figure, particularly popular with young women. When she appeared in Noël Coward's *Fallen Angels* at the Globe in 1925 the press condemned the play as 'vile', 'obscene', 'degenerate', but the show ran for months. In 1928 thousands of female fans mobbed Tallulah on the opening night of *Her Cardboard Lover*, almost overturning her cream Bentley in the rush. She and Joe had a brief affair. 'My family warned me about men,' Tallulah said, 'but they never mentioned women!'

Joe's actress friends hired X Garage cars to ferry them about. Joan Mackern took Gwen Farrar and Norah Blaney to their first BBC broadcast. She also drove Tallulah and Gwen on a treasure hunt round London, which kicked off at Hyde Park Corner and finished at 4 a.m. with breakfast for all at Norfolk

House, St James's Square. Joan, Gwen and Tallulah came in second, ahead of the Prince of Wales, and won £5.

Teddie Gerard, another actress friend of Joe's, appeared in *A-Z* with Bea Lillie and Gertrude Lawrence. 'Miss Teddie Gerard, looking properly scared, stabs a pursuing Chink,' noted one reviewer. A slight, dark woman with Oriental features, Teddie was born Thérèse Théodora Gérard Cabrié in the Argentine in 1892 and worked as a dancer in Paris before the war. She was acquainted with the set of literary and artistic lesbians in London which included Radclyffe Hall and Una, Lady Troubridge. Joe was not part of this, or any, intellectual clique. There is a cursory mention of Joe in Una Troubridge's diary entry of October 30 1923: 'Teddie and Jo Carstairs arrived at 11.30 [p.m.] . . . and stayed til 1.30 when we were glad to see the back of them.'

Joe flourished in the world of action rather than intellect. To her friend and fellow yachtsman Anthony Heckstall-Smith, she was 'the epitome of the twenties. A neat, trim little girl who, with her short cut hair and blue beret worn at a jaunty angle, her flashing white teeth, infectious laugh, was like an exuberant schoolboy with her zest for speed and adventure.' In his memoirs Heckstall-Smith recalled the aftermath of a party on the *Sonia* which he joined off the Isle of Wight after a day racing motorboats.

One of Joe's guests fell overboard quite late at night, when all the boats were up in davits and the crew asleep in the fo'castle. I, too, was sitting below in the saloon, in my pyjamas and dressing-gown, talking to another guest before going to bed, when we heard cries for help. We both dashed on deck.

It was a very dark, rather windy night, with a strong spring tide running through the roads to the westward. In the excitement and the confusion, it was difficult to discover exactly what had happened, for even Joe seemed momentarily unnerved. My companion in the saloon seized a lifebelt and dived over the side while Joe was still for'ard urging the crew to action. I remember running aft and hearing cries of 'Help!' Looking over the stern, I saw one of the guests, Ruth Baldwin, struggling in the water. So in I went, throwing off my pyjamas. Soon the frightened Ruth, who was twice my size, and I were struggling together, and, frankly, I thought she would drown me. As we floundered about, the terrible realisation dawned upon me that Joe had shouted that Mabs, another guest, had fallen overboard. She had said nothing about Ruth. So no one knew that either she or I were in the sea. In that streaming tideway, even had I been alone, to swim back to *Sonia* would have been almost beyond my powers as a swimmer. Supporting the frightened Ruth, it was out of the question. All I could do was to turn on my back and allow the tide to carry us along, farther and farther from the yacht.

How long we were in the water I do not know, but it must have been some considerable time before we were eventually picked up by the launch of a nearby yacht – the *Amphitrite*, owned by Colonel Gage – which was anchored not far from *Sonia* and whose crew had heard our cries for help. By the time the launch reached us, I was practically unconscious. Somehow, in the mêlée, Ruth, too, had parted company with her pyjamas, so the pair of us were stark naked.

Since Colonel Gage was a member of the Royal Yacht Squadron, as soon as I recovered I realised just what a scandal the whole incident would cause in Cowes on the following day.

'Let us,' I said to Joe, who was in my cabin giving me brandy, 'Let us leave for Southampton at dawn. I'm sure you can no more face the gossip and tittle-tattle of the morrow than I can!'

Then I went mercifully to sleep. When I awoke, we were lying off Hythe, and a few hours later, the whole party were speeding to London in two of Joe's fastest motor-cars. Even so, Cowes was agog with the story for weeks to come, and I had quite a hard time explaining how and why Ruth Baldwin and I were drifting about the roads *deshabillées* in the middle of the night. When Colonel Gage suggested that he should recommend me for a medal of some sort or other, I pleaded with him to forget the whole incident.

Joe and Ruth seemed to be forever falling into the water or into trouble, capsizing, bobbing back to the surface. Theirs was a topsy-turvy world, in which women smoked cheroots and drank brandy, lesbians were caught naked with nice young men, dolls paraded as lords and heiresses as mechanics. Joe ploughed her ambulance through the debris of the First World War, and then her motorboat through the debris of the Thames; she delighted in stirring things up, whether the waters of the Solent or the sensibilities of the older generation. It was a bravura performance, like the precarious skimming of a hydroplane: powered by her money, Joe lifted herself clear of censure by dint of nerve and speed.

9

~~~~~~~~~~~~~~

NOBODY REALLY KNOWS ANYTHING
ABOUT THEIR BEHAVIOUR

For fear of sinking, Joe Carstairs did not allow herself to slow: when one of her ambitions was achieved, a new one swiftly replaced it. By 1927 Joe had won the major competitions in the one-and-a-half-litre class, and she set her sights on the most prestigious motorboating prize in the world, the Harmsworth British International Trophy.

Alfred Harmsworth, the proprietor of the *Daily Mail*, had established the competition in 1903, the dawn of high-speed motorboating. The boats entered for the race could be up to forty feet long, and no limit was placed on engine size; as a consequence the contest became a playground for millionaires, and a testing ground for the most powerful and experimental craft of the time. In the first decade of the Harmsworth, the British won the trophy five times, the Americans four times, the French once.

During the war the competition was suspended. It was contested again in 1920 at Osborne Bay, off the Isle of Wight, and was won for America by Garfield Wood in *Miss America*, a boat powered by twin 900hp aircraft engines.

Gar Wood, 'the Grey Fox of Algonac', was to be Joe's great rival. He was a fearless racer and a showman, endlessly, inventively competitive. In the year he first won the Harmsworth he also raced against the Havana Special, the fastest train on the Atlantic coastline, for 1,240 miles from Miami to New York. He beat it by twenty-one minutes. The next day he set out on a 2,300-mile journey up the Hudson to Detroit. Three months later he raced his boat against an aeroplane over sixteen miles of the St Clair river, and beat it by two minutes. His supremacy on the water was absolute. For the next seven years no British racer came near him.

In 1927 Joe commissioned Sam Saunders to build her three boats with which to race against Wood, and one with which to make an attempt on the transatlantic record. The three hydroplanes, constructed in great secrecy, were designed to be the fastest craft ever to travel on water, capable of 100mph; they were reputed to be costing her £50,000. These were the boats that Joe named in memory of her mother, believing her name to be Estelle. 'I thought I'd give her a lift,' she said. By forgetting that her mother was called Evelyn,

Joe exacted a sly revenge. It is a measure of how successfully she had cut her ties with her family that there seems to have been no one around who would know to correct the mistake.

Estelle I, at twenty-six foot by five-and-a-half foot, was shaped like a shark, neat, sleek, with an upward tilt on the blunted point of the nose. *Estelle II* was shorter and fatter, like a small whale. *Estelle III* was never completed – her design had been over-ambitious. The two finished hydroplanes were extraordinarily light, the hulls crammed tight with power. Their thin wooden shells were cases for tremendous 900hp Napier Lion engines, which had already powered record-breaking aircraft and motor cars. Both had turtle-back decks which merged seamlessly into the sides of the hulls, a design which improved the boats' aerodynamism but meant that if overturned they would be difficult to right. Joe unveiled the two *Estelles* at East Cowes in June 1928. 'Nobody really knows anything about their behaviour,' she told the press. 'We are venturing into a new region of speed on the water.'

In the event *Estelle I* proved highly volatile, and sank on her first outing on Windermere. Evidently there were problems with the smaller *Estelle* too, because on 22 July Carstairs pulled out of the Harmsworth. 'I have now had an opportunity of thoroughly testing the British challengers for the Harmsworth Trophy,' she announced. 'After most careful consideration and review of their seaworthiness and safety of their hulls I have reluctantly come to the conclusion that they will not uphold the prestige of Great Britain at this important international event. Please therefore accept withdrawal of my entry.' A week later, though, she heard that one of Gar Wood's boats had been damaged. Armed with the knowledge that his craft too were fallible, she could not resist renewing the challenge: she would race *Estelle II* at Detroit for the 1928 Harmsworth Trophy.

Joe planned to make the 3,000-mile crossing from Cowes to New York in July, at an average speed of 50 to 60mph – the previous year Charles Lindbergh had passed into legend by flying from New York to Paris in a monoplane. Joe's new transatlantic craft, *Jack Stripes*, was a seventy-eight-foot cutter with a bullet-shaped bow designed to break through ocean waves. To ensure that she could withstand a collision with a whale or a submerged shipwreck, her hull was built with five laminations of Consuta copper-sewn Burmese teak and clad with a riveted double-skin of Honduras mahogany. But when Joe took *Jack Stripes* out on the Channel for a test run the boat proved disastrous – she was 'bucking like an insane bronco', Joe said. Sam Saunders sacked F. P. H. Beadle, who had designed the boats, and Joe was forced to surrender her plan to speed across the Atlantic to America.

Joe trained assiduously for the Harmsworth, not

only in the water but also in the gymnasium. For two hours each day she boxed and lifted weights, putting on 10lbs in muscle. In the build-up to the race she drank no alcohol. Then, with Joe Harris, Wadley, Ruth and a group of friends, Joe Carstairs set out from Southampton in August on the Cunard liner *Berengaria*.

The *Berengaria* immediately entered Joe's pantheon. 'It's my ship,' she declared. The boat had been launched in Germany as the *Imperator* in 1912, and handed over to the Allies in 1920 as a part of war reparations. One of the largest ships in the world, she could carry 5,500 passengers; within her great black hull were brightly lit lounges decked out with huge fireplaces, Tudor beams, heavy wooden chairs, antlers on the walls; she was as solid as a German hunting lodge and as airy as a grand hotel.

Once Carstairs reached Detroit, she posed for the press with Wadley. A caption accompanying a picture of her in a local newspaper read: 'A puzzler: Mannish: This picture you might accept as that of a male movie star, might you not? It isn't. It's an excellent likeness of Miss M. B. Carstairs, foremost motor-boat enthusiast in Britain'; another local paper ignored her plainly masculine appearance and obstinately described her as 'the pretty English motor-boat racer'. In the same feminising spirit the press in North America insisted on referring to Joe as 'Betty' in their reports. Presumably this was an innocent mistake which was repeated as reporters drew on one another's articles, but Joe loathed the nickname and claimed that journalists used it out of spite. One American reporter to whom she complained about this practice had to concede that 'anyone who knows the young woman would quite appreciate the ineptness of the title'.

On 2 September, 150,000 spectators gathered to watch the race for the Harmsworth Trophy. An article in the *Detroit Free Press* described what ensued.

With the crack of the starting gun Miss Carstairs shot her boat over the line more than 300 yards in advance of her rivals and thus won the first test of the race. Riding easily and without throwing much spray the English challenger was opened up and it appeared as though Wood was in for the greatest race of his career.

Sensing the test he was being put to, Wood . . . opened up the *Miss America VII* . . . Its two powerful Packard motors roaring and flames shooting a foot out of the exhausts, Wood cut down the margin of the Carstairs craft and passed it just going under the bridge . . .

The English girl was making a real race of it and followed close in the wash of Wood . . . Miss Carstairs . . . made the turn and was heading up the straightaway when, without warning, her boat leaped into the air and plunged nose first into the water throwing both Miss Carstairs and her mechanic out . . .

As the patrol hurried to rescue the unfortunate crew Miss Carstairs waved that she was alright but urged them to hurry to [Joe] Harris whom they found in an almost unconscious state, paddling to keep on top of the water. Miss Carstairs was swimming and watched them lift her stricken helper into the rescue boat and then climbed in with him.

Joe Carstairs said that she would have perished had the hull been riveted together rather than sewn with copper wire: she was shot out of the boat's side the moment it hit the riverbed. When she reached the surface she was still chewing gum. 'Other racing boats were coming at us,' she said. 'I thought we'd get our heads taken off.' Joe Harris was examined by a doctor, who found he had broken two ribs. After dinner that evening it emerged that Carstairs had cracked three of hers, but she went dancing anyway. She later claimed that her American rivals had tried to murder her by deliberately catching her boat in their wash; on other occasions she alleged that they had filled her tank with sugar.

The *Detroit Free Press* paid tribute to Joe Carstairs's prowess on the water: 'While her misfortune was disastrous and came with amazing suddenness,' it noted, 'Miss Carstairs gave a demonstration of piloting ability never before equalled by a woman . . . She outgeneralled Wood.' Joe had established herself as the fastest woman on water anywhere in the world. But this, of course, was not good enough.

Since the boats built by the Saunders yard in 1928 had failed her, Joe Carstairs set up her own boatyard on the Medina river in East Cowes. She named it Sylvia, after a friend, and took on a task force of six men. Joe Harris was the chief engineer, Arthur 'Gubby' Gubbins the foreman, Jimmy Dexter the painter of the boats and Bert Hawker the designer. The work on Joe's next challenger for the Harmsworth was again conducted in secret – high walls were erected around the tiny boatyard, prefiguring the walls with which Joe would surround herself at Whale Cay. The craft under construction was referred to by the press as the 'hush-hush boat', the 'mystery boat' and the 'Q boat'.

When *Estelle IV* was completed in June 1929 Joe took her staff out for a slap-up meal at the Victoria Tavern, a public house next to the yard, before launching the new craft in the Medina. 'Well, that's that,' she said as the boat hit the water, and then, in a characteristically malapropical phrase: 'The rest is on the knees of the gods.' Joe had a careless, confident way with words. Once, when asked for the source of her prodigious energy, she smartly replied: 'Effluvium

— that's what I call it. I don't know if the word's in the dictionary.' Like a child, she played loosely with language, half-indifferent and half-amused by her slips and inappropriate conjunctions.

'Miss Carstairs's boat is one of the cleanest-designed hulls ever seen,' reported the *Manchester Chronicle*, 'with lengthy, beautiful, upswept bows.' *Yachting* magazine praised this 'beautiful boat, 35ft of glistening black hull, well proportioned and with all the elements of speed'. According to the *Daily Telegraph*, she was 'the most wonderful motor boat that has ever been made'. Though graceful and streamlined, *Estelle IV* was a massive, sturdy craft, thirty-five foot long; *Estelle II* had failed, said Joe, because she was too small and light. The new boat's keel was solid English oak, her flanks were Ecuadorean timber, painted on either side with a Union Jack. She was equipped with three Napier Lion 935hp engines, and triple propellers cut from eighty tons of steel.

Thanks to the excitement of the previous year's Harmsworth race, three times as many people – half a million – turned up to watch in Detroit in 1929. *Estelle IV* averaged 64mph in the trials, a new British record. But during the race itself she handled badly and hit a log, loosening a manifold in the engine. Gar Wood triumphed again. 'As far as competition went,' reported *Yachting*, 'this year's widely heralded race for the British International Trophy was a dismal failure.'

To top it all, while being loaded after the race *Estelle IV* slipped from the crane and was damaged.

In October Joe gave an interview to Lillian Sabine of the American magazine *Motor Boating*. Sabine found Joe's 'rollicking boyishness' appealing, and like Anthony Heckstall-Smith saw her not as an oddity but as an embodiment of modernity. 'She has a straightforward manner,' Sabine wrote, 'unaffected and sincere. She is fearlessly honest – in the modern spirit. More than anyone I had ever met, Marion Carstairs seemed to me a product of her generation.'

But Joe's manner was not entirely straightforward. Her desire for visibility was equalled by her desire for concealment, and in order to obscure herself she played 'in the modern spirit' with the idea of fixed identity. In this she was a true child of her time. Towards the end of the interview with Lillian Sabine she called to one of her retinue of girls, 'Bring Lord Tod Wadley in.' Wadley was brought, and Joe solemnly placed him in Lillian Sabine's hand, a token of herself. 'If anything happened,' she said, 'I'd save him first.' Then, further dislocating her identity, Joe Carstairs pointed at one of the other women in the room: 'That's Marion Carstairs.'

10

AN ABSURD MANIKIN

By the late 1920s the tide was turning against the likes of Joe Carstairs. Her vaunted pluck was beginning to be seen as a rebellion against nature. In the immediate aftermath of the war, masculine women were perceived – at worst – as contemporary curiosities but in 1928 the publication of Radclyffe Hall's *The Well of Loneliness* irrevocably sexualised them. The heroine of Radclyffe Hall's novel was, like Joe Carstairs, a well-to-do woman who dressed in men's clothes; like Carstairs, she had served as an ambulance driver in France; and like Carstairs she had a female lover. The book was banned. In a notoriously intemperate leading article, the editor of the *Sunday Express* fulminated against homosexuality.

Bravado

I am well aware that sexual inversion and perversion are horrors which exist among us today. They flaunt themselves in public places with increasing effrontery and more insolently provocative bravado. The decadent apostles of the most hideous and loathsome vices no longer conceal their degeneracy and their degradation.

They seem to imagine that there is no limit to the patience of the English people. They appear to revel in their defiance of public opinion. They do not shun publicity. On the contrary, they seek it, and they take a delight in their flamboyant notoriety. The consequence is that this pestilence is devastating the younger generation. It is wrecking young lives. It is defiling young souls.

The Plague

I have seen the plague stalking shamelessly through great social assemblies. I have heard it whispered about by young men and young women who do not and cannot grasp its unutterable putrefaction. Both aspects of it are thrust upon healthy and innocent minds. The contagion cannot be escaped. It pervades our social life.

Perhaps it is a blessing in disguise or a curse in disguise that this novel forces upon our society a disagreeable task which it has hitherto shirked, the task of cleaning itself from the leprosy of these lepers, and making the air clean and wholesome once more . . .

> The English people are slow to rise in their wrath and strike down the armies of evil, but when they are aroused they show no mercy, and they give no quarter to those who exploit their tolerance and their indulgence.

In the same year the first predatory lesbian – Countess Geschwitz in *Pandora's Box* – was portrayed on screen. A powerful connection was made in the public mind between the 'mannish women' who emerged from the Great War and the masculine 'inverts' who had suddenly come to light.

The medical establishment had acknowledged the existence of sexual love between women in the nineteenth century, and given such women a variety of labels: they were inverts, the intermediate sex, the third sex, urnings, men trapped inside women's bodies. By the 1920s the issue had become more vexed: in *The Psychogenesis of a Case of Homosexuality in a Woman* (1920) Freud attributed lesbianism to rejection by the father, raising the possibility of a psychological 'cure'. Meanwhile the work on glands and grafting conducted by the likes of Serge Voronoff raised the possibility that sexuality was medically adjustable. 'It is not only perfectly possible, but even probable, that maladjusted sex factors may exist in man as in moths,' wrote Julian Huxley in 1922. 'Several results follow, the first the distinct possibility that cases of sexual perversion may be cured by injection or grafting.'

It was feared that lesbianism was an epidemic. In 1929 a woman was imprisoned for having lived as a man, under the name Colonel Barker. 'You have set an evil example,' explained the judge, 'which, were you to go unpunished, others might follow.'

Sportswomen were picked out as indulging in a dangerous, feverish excess. 'Our girls too strenuous,' ran the headline on an article in the *Daily News* in 1929. 'Are they overdoing it at sport? Expert's warning.' The article cautioned that 'Zeal is being allowed to outrun discretion, with serious physical results.' Nominally the subject of the article was sport; but the comment reflected the growing concern about young women's sexual promiscuity and about lesbianism in particular. 'The trouble is "over-keenness",' the piece continued. 'She "gets the fever" . . . It is a jolly life – but it may be a dangerous one.'

By 1930 a sour note was occasionally entering press reports about Carstairs, and her behaviour to reporters had become fractious. Joe may have lost her tolerance for newspapermen when Wadley was described in an American paper as an 'absurd manikin'. Carstairs too was perceived now as a comic or sinister would-be man. Characteristics never mentioned before – her continual gum-chewing, her tattoos, her spitting, her swearing – began to surface in the articles: 'She smokes incessantly,' reported one, 'not with languid feminine grace, but with the sharp decisive gestures a man uses.' *Estelle IV* had been hailed for her clean design and her beautiful bows; when *Estelle V* was launched in 1930 she was described as 'powerful but ugly'. As the heady 1920s gave way to the sober 1930s, Carstairs's verve, independence and experimentation were being interpreted as insalubrious and freakish.

Questions were raised in the press about whether racing itself was healthy: perhaps the desire for speed was a dangerous, insatiable appetite, a sign not of progress but of decadence. Joe began to cast her motorboating – and by implication her sexuality – as a compulsion rather than a choice. 'I wouldn't race,' she told a reporter, 'only I can't help it.' Many racers felt compelled to defend their sport in newspaper interviews and columns, pointing for example to the potential benefits to industry that the development of powerful engines might bring.

Then in June 1930 the national hero Sir Henry Segrave was killed breaking the water-speed record on Windermere. Segrave had been knighted that year after beating Gar Wood in America (in a boat designed, like *Newg*, by Fred Cooper) and he had planned to race for the 1930 Harmsworth, as the first British competitor other than Joe for many years. Carstairs and Segrave were friends as well as rivals, and when he died she was asked for her reaction. 'England has lost a great man and a great champion,' she began, conventionally enough. But then her eulogy turned defensive: 'He was a man of abnormal nerve . . . I never liked these freak boats, such as Sir Henry Segrave had. I have said so before and I am more certain of it now . . . The *Estelle* boats, with which I hope to win the world's championship, are not freaks. They are ordinary.'

Joe went to America in June with *Estelle IV*, which had been rebuilt for the 1930 Harmsworth, and *Estelle V*, a twenty-eight-foot hydroplane. Again she was the only British entrant. She did not attend her own send-off party, a dance on a steamer down the Thames hosted by Ruth Baldwin. 'This will be my third attempt,' Joe announced on reaching the United States, 'and if I do not succeed this time I shall pack it up. Motorboat racing is too expensive to carry on indefinitely.' She was bullish with reporters. 'I want to be treated as a man,' she told one. 'I don't want any allowances made because I'm a woman.'

At the trials on Lake Muskoka in July *Estelle V* broke the American record with a speed of 94.5mph (the world record set by Segrave stood at 98.76mph). But in the race on 1 September, watched by the largest crowd ever gathered for a sporting event, both Joe's boats broke down. At the end of the race she climbed out of her boat and spat. 'Well, you'd better get a good look at me,' Joe told the waiting reporters, 'because I am not coming over again. It's too frightfully expensive.' (Since she was renowned for her uninhibited language, it is possible that this last phrase was cleaned up for publication.) Joe had spent about $500,000 in her several attempts at the Harmsworth. Though she had no traffic with such concepts as regret, fear or failure, she was clearly bitterly disappointed. Out of this disappointment she constructed a curious story.

As she told it, Wadley came close to death days after the race, in a fire at the house they were renting. The house was empty at the time, but a boy spotted the doll on a windowsill in the burning building, and plucked him from the blaze. When Wadley was restored to Joe she rewarded his young saviour with as much ice-cream as he could eat. She had always had a special fondness for boys, and the rescue of Wadley confirmed to her that she and they shared an understanding.

Soon afterwards, Joe said, as the party left their holiday home for the railway station, their motor car spun into a ditch; again Carstairs and Wadley were unscathed.

Joe later claimed that before she left England for America a fortune-teller had predicted that her rivals would attempt to kill her by forcing her boat to crash, that her house would burn down, and that her car would career into a ditch. All these predictions, she said, came true. Newspaper reports confirm that her holiday home near the river caught fire in 1930; the building was destroyed, and Joe helped the fire brigades save other cottages. The motor car accident was not recorded in the press. But the boat crash had taken place two years earlier, during Joe's first attempt at the Harmsworth.

By including the fortune-teller's premonition in her account and by telescoping the sinking of the boat, the fire and the car crash – the triple deliverance from death – Carstairs created meaning out of accident. She gave magic and depth to the story by shadowing her experiences with Wadley's. Told in these terms, her trip to America took on epic proportions: it was shot through not with defeat but with miracles.

Back in England Joe was forced to deal with impertinent questions from the press, which she handled with good grace. 'An attractive young sportswoman smilingly admitted to me this afternoon that she places her career before marriage,' ran one article. 'She is Miss Betty Carstairs, the daring motor-boat racer, whom I had just told of rumours of her engagement. "There is not a word of truth in them," she replied. "I am far too interested in racing to worry about a husband."'

In 1930 Joe gave her friend Malcolm Campbell £10,000 towards building a racing car, *Bluebird*, in which he attained 245mph the next year, breaking his own world land-speed record. On his return to London, Campbell made a triumphal progress to receive his knighthood: he and the mighty *Bluebird* were national icons. Joe had wanted her contribution to *Bluebird* kept secret but somehow it came out, and Campbell publicly thanked her for her generosity. She had been reduced to vicarious success, to the role of wealthy patron rather than action hero – Malcolm Campbell, who had once described Joe Carstairs as 'the greatest sportsman I know', was now thanking her for her money. She had been shifted off the male stage, and into a traditional female position behind the scenes. Betraying her envy of Campbell, Joe later remarked 'usually he drives like an old woman'.

Even the X Garage was no more: it had folded in 1928, driven out of business when Daimler set up its own touring company. In any case, both Bardie Coleclough and Joan Mackern became engaged to be married that year. In 1929 Bardie married Billy Tyrrell, an Irish international rugby player who had been awarded six DSOs in the war, and Joan married a solicitor.

Joe did carry on racing in Britain for a few months, and she continued to meet with disappointment. In an attempt to recapture the glory days, when *Newg* and *Sonia* triumphed in English waters, Joe built a *Newg II* and a *Sonia II*. At the Detroit News Trophy race in 1931 *Newg II* shot out of the water, heeled over and sank, throwing the Joes Harris and Carstairs clear. The same year Joe challenged the French yachtswoman Madame V. Heriot to a 190-mile race from Ryde to the Havre lightship and back: Mme Heriot's *Ailée* beat *Sonia II* by seventeen minutes. Bardie Coleclough recalled this as the only time she saw Joe angry – on the drive home, Joe told Bardie that she was going to emigrate. (Tallulah Bankhead had also had enough of England by 1931, and she returned that year to the United States, leaving her dresser, Kate, to be Joe and Ruth's housekeeper at Mulberry Walk.)

From then on, Joe Carstairs spent little time in Britain – or the public eye. In 1931 Joe, Wadley and Mabs Jenkins, a manicurist with a small green scorpion tattooed on her thigh, set off on a round-the-world voyage. (Mabs had been the other woman to fall overboard on the night that Anthony Heckstall-Smith rescued Ruth Baldwin.) Their visit to India was the highlight of the trip.

'The place calls,' Joe said; it was the place where she believed her father had died. 'Ever since I was a kid I have been used to handling a gun, and I love shooting.' Joe and 'Kip', as she nicknamed Mabs, shot a panther apiece. After Kip's kill the two women were so hot that they went for a swim in a lake thick with crocodiles. 'I do not remember enjoying a swim so much,' Carstairs said. 'It was here I shot the crocodile we shipped home.' Joe shot her panther at twenty-five yards. 'I had the satisfaction of seeing my animal drop right in its tracks,' she boasted. 'It makes you feel bucked at the moment of doing that, you know. It was a male panther, and was one inch under eight feet long.'

Over fifteen months Joe and Mabs visited Cuba, Honolulu, Fiji, New Zealand, Australia, New Guinea, the Dutch East Indies, Bali, Java and Singapore. 'Nothing stopped,' said Joe. 'It went on and on.' A Sri Lankan served as a batman to the two women, and Joe supported him and his family for the rest of his life. When he fell in love, he asked 'the Respected Miss' for permission to marry, and every year he sent her boxes of tea.

After her trip round the world, as if unmoored, Joe travelled back and forth between London, where she still lived with Ruth, and New York, where she lived with Isabel T. Pell, a doctor's daughter and 'a very charming girl I was having a thing with'.

'Ruth didn't like it,' said Joe. 'Ruth used to start throwing her guns around and carrying on. On and on and on and on. She was so drunk most of the time. I don't *think* it was my fault.' Joe's relationship with Ruth had run into trouble. Both women seemed to have lost their bearings, but Ruth, with no Wadley to anchor her, more dangerously so. Ruth, like Joe's mother, was drinking heavily and using drugs – heroin and probably cocaine, which was readily available in London nightclubs.

Having built five vessels to win glory for her country, Joe Carstairs started to use her boats to flee it. 'I will set sail and be a regular sailor,' she told the *New York Times*. 'As a matter of fact, that is what I enjoy being more than anything else. I have no bent for art or for such accomplishments as one usually associates with girls. I love the water, the being a sailor, with the free, soothing sea beneath me.'

She described *Sonia II* as her 'floating home'. A three-masted, 450-ton schooner, *Sonia II* had three bathrooms and an oak-panelled saloon more than sixty feet square. In 1931 Joe took her schooner on a treasure hunt to Cocos Island, 500 miles south-west of Panama, where booty worth $12,000,000 was said to be buried. The Spanish pirate Don Pedro Benito had reputedly hidden his illgotten gains on the island in 1822 and then – like Captain Flint in Stevenson's *Treasure Island* – slain all those who knew its whereabouts. Joe failed to find the treasure, as Malcolm Campbell had before her.

The next year Joe built the *Berania*, a miniature version of her beloved *Berengaria*. Like an ocean liner, the *Berania* housed a cocktail bar, a kitchen, a pantry, a dining saloon, a deck saloon (which served as a dance-floor), three cabins, crew space with cots and a promenade deck. Beneath two of the bunks were huge tanks, each holding 2,500 gallons of fuel. Designed by Fred Cooper and built in the Sylvia Yard, the *Berania* was constructed to withstand heavy weather and to run at speed – she was the fastest and most powerful express motor cruiser in British waters. *Berania* and *Sonia II* were Joe's prototype isles of exile.

In 1933 Joe saw an advertisement in an American newspaper offering for sale an island in the British West Indies. She sailed over to see it. In 1934 she bought Whale Cay for $40,000, and left England for good. She told the press that she was going because of the prohibitive tax rates in Britain. She was receiving about £1,000 a week from her trust funds but she later admitted to friends that she was $100,000 in debt, having paid no taxes at all in Britain or America in the 1920s. She said that her flight to the British West Indies, a tax haven, was her only way of escaping jail. But there were other inducements to go, among them the collapse of her dream to be the fastest motorboat racer in the world, the deterioration of her relationship with Ruth and the growing hostility of the British press and public.

'I am going to live surrounded only by coloured people,' she said. 'I am not even taking a motor car, for when I bought the island there were no roads. Now I am building roads and a residence, but my only means of transport will be two ten-foot dinghies. The island is about 1,000 acres in extent and is nine miles long. I cannot say if I will ever return.'

Again Joe pre-empted her own abandonment, rejecting those who seemed on the brink of rejecting her. 'I
want to be left alone,' she told the press. 'There was
a time when I couldn't live my own life, could not
get away from publicity. Well, that's over.'

11

<hr>

FAINT HEART NEVER
WON FAIR LADY

When Joe Carstairs first set eyes on Whale Cay, the force of her feelings animated the island, imbued it with her own desire. Joe claimed it beckoned to her. 'Come on,' urged Whale Cay, 'I want you.'

'This island', Joe maintained, 'had a particular liking for me.'

The British West Indies, as the Bahamas were then known, lay off the coast of Florida. In the late nineteenth century Gordon Lewis, a British writer, described the archipelago as 'a forgotten, derelict corner of the world'. Not much had changed.

The people of the Bahamas had always lived off the sea, not only as fishermen but as pirates in the eighteenth century and as wreckers since the seventeenth: ships frequently foundered on the shallow rocks and reefs, and the islanders were adept at plundering their shells. From the 1840s Bahamians also farmed the reefs for sponges for export, and in the 1920s, during the American Prohibition, many worked as rum-runners. The people's lives were so governed by the wind and the sea that they spoke of the islands, like ships, as having windward and leeward sides: to windward, tenacious vines and shrubs clung to the stony edge; to leeward, mangrove thickets rose from the water, a dark green tangle.

In 1930 the 700 islands were populated by 60,000 people, 50,000 of them black. The ruling class of whites lived in Nassau, New Providence, the capital of the colony; the other islands and cays, known as the Out Islands, were inhabited almost entirely by blacks.

By the mid-1930s a serious depression had descended on the British West Indies. Since the United States had repealed its prohibition law in 1933 the rich trade in smuggling alcohol to the southern states had collapsed. Fewer ships were passing through the archipelago, so there were also fewer wrecks. The sponge trade was declining through overfishing. The United States, meanwhile, countered its own unemployment problem by tightening immigration restrictions, so closing another means by which Bahamians could escape poverty. And between 1926 and 1932 a series of strong storms and hurricanes had hit the islands, devastating crops and settlements. On the Out Islands there were cases of death by starvation.

Whale Cay was one of the thirty Berry Islands, thirty miles north-west of Nassau and ninety miles east of Miami. When Joe arrived the cay was inhabited by a black couple who tended the lighthouse. Joe asked them whether they lit the beacon every night, and they replied, to her amusement, 'Only when the weather's good.'

Joe was not the first white person to try to tame Whale Cay. She said that the original settler was a young favourite of Queen Victoria's, who was sent there when he ran into political trouble towards the end of the nineteenth century. Joe liked to compare her situation to his. 'I was an exile,' she said. In 1906 the island was bought by a Mr Wilde, who tried to farm sisal, a fibrous plant used for ships' rope, and built himself a house from mud and wine bottles. But his business did not flourish and he abandoned the cay. Then a hotel group tried and failed to develop Whale Cay as a holiday resort; one of its members was said to have killed himself in the house built by Mr Wilde. In the 1920s, when alcohol was banned in the United States, Americans took day-trips from Florida to the island to attend rum-drinking parties hosted by Harold Christie, the leading real-estate developer in the British West Indies. Once Prohibition ended the island lost its value as a drinking resort, and it was Christie who sold Whale Cay to Joe.

'When I saw the island I thought this is what I must

do,' Joe said. 'Something great will come of it.' In the year that she took up residence there H. M. Bell wrote in *Isles of June*, his book about the British West Indies, that the colony was 'above all a man's land – giving him back stoutness of spirit, bringing out the pioneer worth that lies hidden in us all'. Joe had to battle to master her island, but this made the prize the more precious: 'I don't think anything is worthwhile unless you fight for it,' she said. 'Faint heart never won fair lady.'

The islands of the British West Indies were the flattened peaks of a giant submarine mountain rising out of the Atlantic Ocean. Joe Carstairs was god of her own portion of this watery Olympus. And to live on Whale Cay was virtually to live in the sea. Its land, which had once been sea-bed, was oolitic limestone, formed by the compacted skeletons of billions of marine creatures. Nine miles long and four miles wide, the cay rose gently from the waters around it; off the shore at the northern end the ocean floor dropped suddenly to 6,500 ft. Low hills, made of sand blown up by the ocean winds, sat at the northern tip of the cay and white beaches circled the coast. The sea around them teemed. Coral reefs, visible through the light water, lay off the beaches, and shoals of fish swarmed through this living rock – grunts, porgies, red snappers, groupers, parrot fish, angel fish. Further out swam blue-fin tuna, dolphins, barracudas and sharks.

The island's surface was thick with grasses and low

jungle. The sisal planted by Mr Wilde had grown straggly and tall. Joe hired seven men from Nassau to help her clear a path and lay road from one end of the island to the other.

'The natives didn't like work,' Joe said. 'They didn't know anything about this kind of work. They had to be shown in detail each step they took. On top of that it was unbearably hot. We wallowed in dust to our knees. Sand flies and other insects bit us almost to the point of distraction. I almost surrendered the island there and then. But I'm stubborn.'

Carstairs, dressed always in khaki, worked alongside the roadlayers – they squatted down to break up the rock with tiny mallets while she climbed trees for a view of where the road should run. The way through the bush was cleared by an old man on a small tractor who chewed his way through three cigars a day. The only other vehicle on Whale Cay in the early days was a red Ford pick-up truck. Later Joe rode a red motorcycle round the island, from which she would holler to her workers: 'Climb on, fellows!'

One morning, Joe said, she and the roadlayers were taking their lunch by the track – she ate oranges, they rice and peas – when she slipped a knife from her belt and hurled it at a snake. 'And by God I cut that goddamn snake's head right off.' The men were deeply impressed, and from then on all the islanders called

Joe 'The Boss'. 'I was a leader,' said Joe. 'I could do anything.'

Joe Carstairs's arrival was a godsend to many. As the buildings of Whale Cay went up and the roads went down people poured in from neighbouring islands. In all, twenty-six miles of carefully signposted road were laid. The first building to be raised was the store. There the workers used their wages – $4 a week for men, $3 for women – to buy lard, rice, sugar, tea and coffee with which to supplement their diet of fish. For refrigeration a large hole was dug on the island and filled with blocks of ice brought over from the mainland by boat.

To begin with, Joe and her friends lived in Mr Wilde's leaky, termite-ridden house at the northern end of the island. 'When it rained,' she recalled, 'it rained in every room.' Joe walked the length of the cay each day to supervise the construction of the Great House at the southern tip. She had hired an architect to design the house but soon dispensed with him – 'He had too many ideas.' The foreman was an American, Mickey Moore: 'A bit of a drunkard,' Joe said, 'but a marvellous man . . . Small, tough, with a shaved head, very anti-black.'

'Mr Moore made reference to my wife under her skirt,' one of the men complained to Carstairs. For this Joe chastised Mickey Moore. '*I* could curse them,' she later explained. 'They took it from me. But not from

Mr Moore.' Joe and Mickey Moore lunched together on dried herring and coffee made with brackish water from the island wells. In the evenings Mickey Moore retired to his shack, which he shared with a big white cat. Joe too brought a large cat to Whale Cay to deal with the mice and rats in the store. The cats mated, and soon scores of their progeny roamed over the island.

Eventually three hundred men were working on the Great House, poling sacks of cement up the river by barge and making concrete blocks reinforced with steel. The house was completed in 1936. It resembled a sturdy Spanish villa, white, with red tiles and wrought-iron railings, and the lawns were planted with palm, tamarind, almond and sea grape trees; the walls surrounding the estate were lined with bushes of oleander, hibiscus and mastik. There were five bedrooms, five large bathrooms, a cold room for meats, a laundry, a dining room, a living room, a kitchen. All were hung with copper ships' lanterns. There were fans to cool the hot winds, and a huge fireplace to warm the main room when it grew cold. Beneath the house was a cistern holding 75,000 gallons of water, so it sat like a liner on its own private sea. The natives lived in shacks in Buckle Cut, a stretch of land adjoining the walled enclosure of the Great House, or on the boats in which they had sailed to the island.

Joe cleared the coconut groves, which had been choked with weeds, and planted 3,000 new palms.

The land was fertilised with humus and irrigated with rainwater stored in huge cisterns. The men sowed fruit and vegetables in pockets of soil among the rocks and they cultivated fields. The women were assigned to pull up weeds on the roads – they became known to Joe and her entourage as weeders or weedresses. Joe did not approve of women labourers: 'If there weren't so many lazy men, women wouldn't have to go to work.' But not all the men were indolent, Joe soon found. She chose her favourites, among them Harry Johnson, who was put in charge of the store, and Jim Moncur, the cook in the Great House.

Joe rebuilt the lighthouse on Whale Cay, fitting it with an electric beacon, and put up a power plant, a radio station, a schoolhouse (on the peak of a hill near the dock) and a circular museum. The island granary, chock-full of corn and guinea corn as well as coconuts, was among the biggest in the Bahamas. Joe experimented with canning fish, with kippering the goggle (herring) and with making fertiliser from fish by-products. She reared pigs and chickens, which at first laid fishy eggs because they ate so many land-crabs.

Joe bought more islands – Bird Cay, Cat Cay, Devil's Cay, half of Hoffman's Cay, a tract of land on the huge island of Andros sixty miles away – and established plantations of canteloupes, potatoes, celery, strawberries, asparagus, bananas, carrots, rice and unusually large peanuts. The Andros farm was the most successful: the small plots of deep soil were protected against rain and flood by terraces of loose stone and against the scorching sun by blankets of pine needles.

Joe acquired a former rum-running cruiser, *Vergemere III*, with which to dredge the beaches and make a harbour at the north end of the island. Once the harbour was built, *Vergemere III*, *Sonia II* and *Berania* were joined by new boats: *Whale* and *Little Doctor* were fishing boats, *Elsa* a speedboat and *Sophie* a launch. In a barn by Shipyard Point Joe had her men build an eighty-five-foot schooner, *Vergemere IV*, which she helped design. The boats' captains included a Captain Cooke, who Joe brought over from England and whose family she supported for fifty years after he left her service. *Estelle IV* was put up on stays by the dock, as a relic, and the engines of *Estelle II* lay by her.

For several years only boats in distress could draw Joe Carstairs out of her seclusion. In December 1937 she summoned the Miami coast guard when a yacht full of American schoolboys ran aground on Whale Cay. The *New York Times* ran a news story on the incident: 'Lt F. A. Erickson, a Coast Guard flier from the Miami station who landed at Whale Cay, her island kingdom, for directions, reported that a girl garbed in men's clothing, who gave the name of B. Carstairs, and a man named Albury had guided him to the vessel.'

Sam Albury was Joe's manager. Bob Coleclough, the brother of Bardie and Molly, had come out as manager in 1934 but he could stomach neither the isolation nor the circling sharks. After a few months he and Joe had a row and he left. Joe seems to have forgiven him, though – she gave Bostwick, her estate in Hampshire, to Bob and his wife, and in 1939 offered to shelter their children on the island as war evacuees.

Ruth Baldwin refused to live on Whale Cay – life there was too primitive and isolated for her tastes. But she visited from a holiday home Joe bought her near Miami; in Ruth's house was a bar named the Wadley Arms, with Wadley's likeness beaming out from a wooden sign hanging over the door. In the early days Joe's girlfriend on the island was Addison, a white woman who one islander remembered as being 'like Miss Carstairs, like a man'; she also made exquisite jewellery. But Addison 'doped awfully', Joe said, and became increasingly difficult to live with. Sometimes Joe found herself in the unlikely position of taking refuge in Ruth's house in Florida.

By the late 1930s more than 200 black men and women were living permanently on Whale Cay, overseen by a small white coterie. Besides Albury, the two men who helped Joe run the island were John Howcroft and Hugh Brooke, known as Tim. Joe had come across John when he was playing the saxophone on the *Berengaria*. 'John was so pretty', she said, 'that

I took him for my own.' John adored Joe, and proved profoundly loyal – it was he who was dispatched to turf Ruth Baldwin out of sailors' bars in Miami. But whatever Joe liked to believe, John was not her own: unlike Wadley, he was not a talisman. Joe found it difficult to share John, and at about the time of his first marriage they fell out; they were eventually reconciled.

Tim Brooke, a writer, joined Joe on the island in 1934. In 1930 he had published the well-received novel *Man Made Angry*, and in his first year on Whale Cay he wrote *Saturday Island*, about the relationship between a boy and a woman shipwrecked together. The book seems to be set on Whale Cay; a map on the inside cover shows a long, narrow island marked with such place-names as Trafalgar Square, Southampton Harbour, Balmoral and Kensington Gardens – Tunbridge Wells is a small outcrop off the coast. Tim was a drinker and a prankster, always ready to join in Joe's games. In sketches the two of them devised for guests on the island, Joe, like a man in drag, would play such emasculating heroines as Salome and Cleopatra.

Once the Great House was built, Joe received a steady stream of friends from England and America, sometimes twenty at a time. Old friends such as Malcolm Campbell, Mabs Jenkins and Bardie Coleclough came. Tallulah Bankhead came, as did Louisa Carpenter du Pont Jenney, a markedly butch lesbian and heiress to a large portion of the du Pont fortune, Marti Mann, later a leading light in Alcoholics Anonymous, and Mercedes de Acosta, a witch-like woman who had affairs with both Greta Garbo and Marlene Dietrich. Joe found Mercedes extremely irritating, particularly when she mooned over one of Joe's girlfriends; the girlfriend remembered Joe shoving Mercedes into an amphibious plane at the end of her stay.

On the cay Joe slept with a series of women she met on her annual trips to New York or Europe or on excursions to Miami. 'I've never had to go out and race and win,' she said. 'They just fall in my lap.' Few were kept on for long: after a while Joe would find herself thinking, 'Oh, God, I've got to go to bed with her again.' Some she had trouble getting rid of. In one case, Joe palmed off a girlfriend on a Hollywood film star who needed to marry as a cover for his homosexuality. But she kept photographs of all her conquests. Was she a great lover? a friend asked her. 'I was made to think so. Everybody else thought so, so I thought so too. I would have liked me.' So she was sensational in bed? 'Oh yes.'

Though Joe herself drank little and took no drugs, her parties were riotous. She also laid on films, rented and home-made, poker games, boxing matches and expeditions to hunt birds and wild goat on neighbouring islands. Joe would take her guests to see the Blue Hole, a thirty-five foot crater at Hoffman's Cay, or to swim off Devil's Cay. They had the run of Whale Cay: there were cars to choose from, and a beach for every wind. (The black workers had their own beach: 'We couldn't have them all over the place,' Joe explained.) Joe staged fishing competitions with cash prizes. She would return from a couple of hours at sea with enough fish to feed the island; the barracudas and sharks were hung under the fruit trees.

In 1936 Joe Carstairs' racing trophies – valued at £900 – were stolen from Mulberry Walk, where Ruth was still living for most of the year. Soon afterwards Joe visited London. She seemed angry, noted the *Daily Sketch*. 'When I left England everyone imagined the most extraordinary things,' Joe told the newspaper. 'Why, I can't think. People seemed to think that there must be some reason for my leaving the country. As if I can't live where I like! I don't like living in England. I am a British subject with an American mother but I do not count myself as British. I prefer now to call myself a colonial – a West Indian.' Her fury seems to have stemmed from the suggestion that she had been driven out of England; she conveniently forgot that in 1934 she had claimed that the rate of taxation, if nothing else, had forced her to leave. (She did not finish paying off the taxes she owed until 1945.)

As if to make clear that it was she who was shutting the world out, and not the world which had excluded her, Joe surrounded all the buildings on Whale Cay with walls. 'I just liked it,' she said. 'Everything had a wall around it.' Yet the walls were statements of authority as much as withdrawal. In building her miniature kingdom she not only banished the outside world but demanded its respect.

12

~~~~~~~~~~

THEY THOUGHT I WAS
MOST UNUSUAL

The West African men and women shipped to the West Indies as slaves since the seventeenth century had brought with them their faith in obeah, a form of voodoo. At the heart of obeah was a belief in the power of the obeah-woman or man, known also as the bush-doctor, and the fetishes he or she wielded. These could work good or evil, swelling a man till he burst or curing him of illness. Carstairs banned obeah on Whale Cay – she, after all, was the dominating spirit of the island – but she could not have failed to understand its power: in many ways the structures of obeah were similar to those which sustained her.

Though obeah was illegal, it was still widely practised in the British West Indies. In 1938 the *Nassau Tribune*, one of the two leading Bahamian newspapers, reported the case of Dorothy Gordon of the island of Eleuthera, a fifteen-year-old girl from whose nostrils small glass crystals were reputedly issuing.

Dr Fields was called . . . and medical science had an explanation for the unusual disorder, but when the neck of a beer bottle came out of the woman's chest and the bottom and side of a gin bottle literally oozed out of her breast, it presented a major phenomenon that no science could explain.

The woman came to Nassau last week, soon after this attack, and the Commissioner has brought a collection of the glass to the city on this trip. This strange incident was also witnessed by a Mr W. B. Johnson, Government Tomato Inspector, who has just returned from Eleuthera . . .

'She tells me that she passed a piece of lamp chimney from the centre of her head at Tarpum Bay two years ago,' said the Commissioner. 'Her mother says that she has passed as high as 50 pieces of glass in one spell. I don't know about this . . . The woman claims that she got a dose of obeah that was set for her mother.'

The inhabitants of Whale Cay practised obeah. A young black boy who was close to Joe grew so jealous of one of the maids in the Great House that he was said to have 'hexed' her, forcing her to flee the island.

Joe Carstairs, with her cherished doll, was the closest thing to an obeah-woman on Whale Cay. Wadley was always at her side – in her boats, in the truck, on the motorbike – and the people suspected he had magical properties. They said the doll was her witchcraft man, able to discover and disclose their secrets. Joe was so strong and fearless that it seemed she was charmed, that a mystery protected her. 'I couldn't figure it out,' reflected one Bahamian who lived on Whale Cay. 'That was her idol, right?' If Joe encouraged such beliefs, she did not need to dissemble to do so: she believed herself supernaturally blessed and she suspected that Wadley was charged with magic. As a friend observed, 'Wadley was her religion.'

Among Joe's favourite books was *The White Witch of Rosehall*, a novel by Herbert G. de Lisser first published in 1929. Based on a true story, it is set in a Jamaican slave plantation almost exactly a century before Joe bought Whale Cay. The 'White Witch' of the title is Annie Palmer, a 'sort of woman hermit' who owns the Rosehall estate. 'She always felt that in England she would count for but little; there would be no supremacy for her there. In Jamaica there was. Here she could live alone, almost unfettered, the life she loved, a life of domination and sensuality. Here she could put to proof the powers she possessed and of which she was inordinately proud.' Annie Palmer bans obeah among her people, only to practise it herself in order to work her will. She is 'white, lovely, imperious, strong, fearless . . . just the sort of girl that a superstitious people would have worshipped . . . and regarded as a sort of goddess . . . Annie came to believe that she possessed the power of a god.' Annie strides about her land brandishing a heavy riding whip (Joe too was said to carry a riding crop) and takes pleasure in watching slaves being flogged. When she conducts her magic rites she dresses 'all in black and like a man'. Annie Palmer also shared with Joe Carstairs a horror of boredom. 'Hell must be a place of utter boredom,' Annie says, 'which is the worst torment a soul can endure.'

'Dull', Joe said, 'is a word that should be torn to pieces to see what it is made of.' To ensure life was never dull, Joe created her own myths, using theatre and practical jokes to at once parody her image and to increase its power. 'It amused her very much to play with people,' said one of her girlfriends. Joe was always stirring up fun and trouble. Often she tricked her house guests, making them believe themselves an audience when they were truly players in her theatre. One night Joe briefed a group of islanders to shine up their faces, strip down to their shorts and drum menacingly outside the Great House. She then told her friends inside that the natives were rioting. 'The blacks are going to kill us all,' she warned. 'Pansies first, women last.' Having whipped up a suitable panic, and sent her guests scuttling upstairs, she strode out and shot off some guns. Then she returned to the house. 'I think it's going to be all right now,' she said.

The Bishop of Nassau visited Whale Cay to dedicate the church in 1938. Joe had a series of pistol shots fired outside his window at one in the morning, and was impressed that he never made mention of the incident.

In the guest bedrooms in the Great House she pinned up a sign:

NOTICE TO GUESTS

(1) USE LIGHT SWITCH ONLY WHEN STANDING ON RUBBER MAT PROVIDED.

(2) ALL VISITORS WISHING MORNING TEA IN THEIR ROOMS WILL BE DEALT WITH ACCORDINGLY.

(3) IT IS DESIRABLE FOR GUESTS TO SLEEP UNDER THE BEDS AS THE MANAGEMENT CANNOT BE HELD RESPONSIBLE FOR ANY DETRIMENTAL INCONSISTENCIES THEREIN.

(4) PLEASE REFRAIN FROM USING BUZZER PROVIDED. SERVANTS RESTING FROM 8 a.m. UNTIL 10 p.m.

(5) ANY OLIVE PITS, RAZOR BLADES, SAFETY DEPOSIT BOXES, OR WINCHELLS COLUMNS LEFT IN BEDS ONLY CONFUSE THE STAFF. KLEENEX IS PROVIDED FOR THESE PURPOSES.

(6) IGNORE CALENDAR. THE MANAGEMENT
    DOES NOT COINCIDE WITH ANNIVERSARIES.

(7) DO NOT DISTURB MOTHS IN CLOTHES
    CLOSET. HATCHING SEASON.

(8) DO NOT PUT CLOTHES IN BUREAU
    DRAWERS. NEVER MIND WHY.

(9) AVOID LOOKING AT PICTURES. IMMORAL!

The notice – anarchic, absurd – was designed to amuse as much as disconcert. But Joe could be righteous and her games could be correspondingly sadistic. When a rich friend of hers took a job in a prestigious New York department store, Joe was outraged by what she saw as injustice – she felt that the post should have gone to someone who needed the money. Joe visited the shop in the guise of a Russian countess (she could adopt immaculate foreign accents), accompanied by Tim Brooke and an Italian man dressed in black suits and hats. While being served by her friend, who did not recognise her through the layers of make-up, Joe suddenly announced that her emerald ring had vanished. The store was turned upside down, and when Joe eventually 'found' her ring she continued to insist that the assistant had tried to steal it. Her friend was sacked.

Joe loved to dress up as a woman. For fancy-dress parties she would wear frumpy dresses and ludicrously vivid make-up, and for shopping excursions in New

York donned a blonde wig, a chiffon dress, a fur stole and high heels. 'To her, that was the epitome of a costume,' said a friend. At the Elizabeth Arden beauty salon in Miami one day, Joe snatched the lingerie from a mannequin and pulled it on over her khaki shirt and trousers, then pulled the dummy's wig on to her own head. Decked out in these, she went into the street and paraded herself, poker-faced.

She also enjoyed putting on the costume of a doctor. In the 1940s Joe had a strikingly beautiful girlfriend she nicknamed 'Cow' or 'Cowley', supposedly for her even temper; Joe in turn was 'Dockle', for her love of doctoring. At a fancy-dress party on Whale Cay, Carstairs enacted a tableau of their relationship: dressed as a doctor, in a stovepipe hat and Abraham Lincoln beard, she led into the room a real cow (when this cow died it was buried on the island, with a tombstone reading 'Cowley Really'). At another party the human 'Cowley' herself popped out of a chest entirely naked, playing *The Flight of the Bumblebee* on a flute. Imitation cows – of cloth, of fur, of china – filled the shelves of their home, some of them accompanied by miniature doctors. One toy cow in particular was worn thin with Joe's kisses.

It is curious that Joe liked to play the doctor, taking on the profession of the hated Serge Voronoff, her mother's fourth husband. But then, one way or another, she modelled herself on all her mother's husbands: Roger de Perigny was a promiscuous play-boy who drove fast cars; and in setting up a private regiment on Whale Cay with herself as ruler, Joe emulated Albert Carstairs and Francis Francis, both colonial army officers.

By claiming for herself the power to heal, Joe became a kind of bush-doctor on the island. For six weeks she even captained a ship round the Windward Islands helping the Red Cross to administer medical treatment. Joe's miniature hospital on Whale Cay was named Estelle, in memory of her mother's work as a nurse in the Boer and Great Wars (Joe had not yet discovered Evelyn's real name). Though Joe had some medical supplies and books and a rudimentary knowledge of medicine from her service with the Red Cross in the First World War, she operated mainly by faith. 'They had a great belief in me,' she explained, 'they thought I was most unusual.'

One woman, a weeder, came to her complaining of heart trouble. 'I will cure you,' said Joe. She gave the woman Peptobismol, and her condition rapidly improved. The weeder would come to dance for the Boss in gratitude. 'You've brought me from the grave,' she exclaimed. Other cures were less mysterious: Joe and an island woman cured a man who had been constipated for six weeks by administering six enemas. 'Let's operate!' was one of Carstairs' favourite rallying cries.

Obeah-men and women were said to be able to discover and punish thieves and adulterers, and Joe's success in detecting and dealing with troublemakers was astonishing. She enjoyed recounting stories to this effect. Every March, she said, a restless violence took hold of her people, and she regularly had to break up fights. In 1940 she threw 150 people off the island after a particularly rowdy dance.

One Saturday evening Carstairs heard there was again trouble at the store, where a dance was being held, and she went over from the Great House with a large torch. The people were cowering indoors: a man with a knife was outside, they told her, complaining that he had been charged too much for beer – 'He's coming in to cut us.' She told them to open the doors at once, and found outside a small, very dark man dressed in a sailor suit and brandishing a penknife. 'Look, my good chap,' she said, 'you come over to me and I'll smash you across the bloody face with this torch. That'll be a damn sight worse than what you can do with that stupid little penknife.' She then ordered that he be removed from Whale Cay and dropped on an island far away. One of the islanders agreed, with belated gallantry: 'We're not going to have the Boss cut to pieces.'

'He's not going to cut anyone to pieces,' Joe returned. 'He's going to have his face smashed in.'

On another occasion a man came to tell the Boss

that all his savings had been stolen from a suitcase under his bunk, and she summoned to her the man she suspected of the crime. Had he stolen the money? Joe asked him. 'Let Jesus come down and strike me with lightning, I didn't,' he replied. 'You're a bloody liar,' said Joe, and unleashed a stream of foul language. At this the suspect produced a board with a nail in it, and threatened Joe. She pulled a knife from her back pocket. 'What are you doing with that board?' she said. 'You come a step nearer and I'll stick this in your gut.' He dropped the board and returned the stolen money.

At 7 a.m. one morning Joe discovered that her safe had been axed open and all the money for the islanders' weekly wage stolen. She made an announcement to her populace. 'Every house including mine will be ransacked,' she told the people. 'No one will get any food until the money is found. No questions asked. People will starve, that's all.' At noon a young man came forward to say he had found the money, bundled up in paper bags and deposited in the scrub land. 'Well done,' said Joe. 'Whoever stole it, he can go in peace. At one o'clock the whistle will blow and you'll go back to work.'

Each morning all islanders with problems or griev-ances would line up outside the Great House and wait for Joe to emerge from breakfast, the most important meal of her day. She would listen to

147

the complaints, which often concerned fights over beer or women, and pass judgement or take action as appropriate. Adultery was punished severely. Joe disapproved of sex outside marriage. She presided over scores of weddings on the island and provided married couples with small, neat houses, while single men lived in barracks. Adulterers were usually banished from Whale Cay, but in at least one instance, in 1939, Joe had the culprit horse-whipped; he complained to the British government but it ruled that whoever owned an island in the dominion was effectively judge and jury over the people. Joe, meanwhile, was seducing a succession of girlfriends in the Great House. The apparent hypocrisy may be explained by Joe's distaste for heterosexual sex; or by her disgust at her mother's adulterous betrayals; or by her belief that she was simply different, above law and morality. Joe was less hard on men who beat their wives. Sometimes she fined them. She tore up a letter from Nassau informing her that this was illegal.

Most inhabited Out Islands were provided with a police force but Joe appointed her own law enforcers: four guards armed with sawn-off shotguns and a watchman with a machete. She was the chief protector of the island. In 1940 Damon Runyon wrote in his syndicated newspaper column about a friend of his who had stopped at Whale Cay in his amphibious plane. 'He came back in a big hurry, reporting in some alarm that when he landed in the water there was a short, stock-built dame came popping out of a house on the cay with a double-barrelled shotgun in her dukes and dull menace in her lovely orbs.'

The Whale Cay museum, known also as the library, was like a pagan shrine. There Joe's life was represented not in words but in the objects she had gathered. The museum housed her racing trophies, the heads of the big game she had shot, the carcasses of the fish she had caught, a life-size statue of Wadley, models of ships and the appendix of Joe Harris. Joe Carstairs expressed regret at having mislaid a necklace of dried human ears, a gift to her mother from an African chieftain she had nursed. There were two brass shell-casings dating from the First World War and engraved with Joe's father's name, Albert. When the island dog, John, died, Joe had him stuffed and put in the museum. She occasionally threatened her employees with a similar fate.

The most impressive display in the library-museum was Joe's large collection of knives – cutlasses, swords, spears, daggers, machetes. She knew the provenance of every one, she boasted, even though they didn't have a word written on them. Joe always carried an English knife, with her comb, in a back pocket. She was precise about this knife's measurements: it was three inches long when closed but when snapped open was a full six inches. Joe carried the knife even when posing for nude photographs. Sometimes, like a pirate, she clenched it between her teeth. At one party on Whale Cay all the guests were naked except Joe, who wore just a hunting knife strapped around her thigh.

When intruders landed on Whale Cay, Joe had free rein in her self-inventions and she sent herself up wildly. One day in the late 1940s, it was said, an American cruiser moored off the island, and its passengers rowed up to the shore, disembarking at Cowley beach. On hearing of the instrusion Carstairs had her men paint their faces and armed them with weapons from the museum. Led by Joe, who was wielding a huge cutlass, they swarmed out of the jungle uttering strange cries and took the trespassers prisoner. At dusk the Americans were dragged up to the lighthouse, their hands tied behind their backs. There Joe reappeared, dressed as a fantastical Great White Goddess, while her people chanted and danced around a huge fire before her. After the ceremony the Americans were locked in the garage; they were released at dawn.

The tourists would have returned from the island excitedly recounting their terrible adventure: the scene of white witchery and black savagery, their night in thrall to a madwoman. But Joe Carstairs' account of the episode would have made the better story, the funnier story, and in it the trespassers are doubly victims —

frightened in their own minds, ridiculed in hers. She loved an audience, not least because the joke, in the end, was at the audience's expense.

Wadley, of course, was a wonderful prop for Joe's practical jokes and for her myth-making. But in her love for him, if nothing else, she was quite serious. She talked to toys so that she could toy with people.

'I was never entirely honest to anyone,' she confessed later in her life, 'except to Wadley.'

13

ALAS, NOW DEAD, THE BED SAID

In August 1937 Ruth Baldwin collapsed at a party in Chelsea after listening to the broadcast of a boxing match; Dolly Wilde was a fellow guest at the party. Ruth was taken to her rooms at Mulberry Walk, just a block away, where she died of a suspected drug overdose.

Ruth was thirty-two, even younger than Joe's mother had been when she died in similar circumstances. A friend once asked Joe whether Ruth had been like Evelyn. 'No, not *at all*,' said Joe. 'No, no, no, no. No. They were both brilliant women, but no, no. Not at all.'

On hearing of Ruth's death, Joe and Tim Brooke crossed the Atlantic to England on the French liner *Normandie*, which at the time of her launch in 1935 was the most expensive ship in the world; her promenades were as wide as streets and the passenger lounge as tall as a three-storey building. Joe left so hastily that she forgot to pack a divided skirt, and since women in trousers were not admitted to the main dining-room she and Tim were obliged to hire a room in which to eat. They spent the six-day voyage drunk.

Joe had ordered that Ruth's body be embalmed, and when she reached Mulberry Walk she saw her fiery girlfriend transformed briefly into a doll-like creature, lifeless and composed. She filled Ruth's room with flowers and sat Wadley at her head. Ruth Baldwin was taken to the Golders Green crematorium and cremated on 7 September.

On Whale Cay, Joe built an Anglican church of native limestone as a memorial to Ruth. Joe believed in God, a God who guided her knife when she chopped off the snake's head, who saved her and Wadley from death by fire or drowning. 'I think there is a higher power who looks after me,' she said. The Church of St Catherine (Catherine was Ruth's first name) was fitted with exquisite stained-glass windows by Alice Laughlin, which were exhibited in New York before being installed. The altar, handcarved in island mahogany, was copied from an altar on the *Normandie*, at which Joe had perhaps prayed on the crossing to England. A memorial service for Ruth was held each year, and an urn containing her ashes was kept in a corner. 'Ruth was the first person who really meant anything to me,' Joe said. 'And, of course, she gave me Wadley.' Joe cried for Ruth – it was, she said, the first time she cried in her life.

Over the next few years many of Joe's friends of the 1920s and 1930s died prematurely. There were exceptions. But Mabs Jenkins, with whom Joe had toured the world in 1931, died in Africa of thyroid problems in the early 1940s, having made a suicide attempt a few years before. Joe's theatre friends Teddie Gerard and Gwen Farrar both died in the same period, Teddie at fifty-two and Gwen at forty-four. Isabel T. Pell, with whom Joe had an affair in the early 1930s, 'died of drink'. 'Why did they all end so badly?' Joe asked.

In 1941 Dolly Wilde too died; officially, the cause was cancer. In 1939, eighteen months after Ruth's death, Joe had lent 5 Mulberry Walk to Dolly for a few days; Dolly seems to have been convalescing, possibly after one of the two suicide attempts she made in the 1930s. 'A lovely, comfortable flat,' she wrote. 'A big bedroom with morning sun streaming in through the windows, splintering its shafts of light on to the mirror.' In the years since Joe had known Dolly her life had steadily declined.

'She could still glitter for her public,' recalled Bettina Bergery, 'but if one came across her unexpectedly, sitting alone at a café table at Les Deux Magots, one was shocked by the apathetic look that so recalled the hopeless apathy of the broken poet Oscar, just before his end.'

Joe had shared with Dolly and Ruth a refusal to look

forwards or backwards, 'that rare and spontaneous quality', in the words of Natalie Barney, 'of living entirely in the moment, with hardly a thought for the past and only a shudder towards the future.' But in the years that followed Ruth's death Joe began to remember and to record: she started to write poetry. It was a short-lived period of introspection, and an odd one in the life of a woman who claimed 'I never felt anything *about* myself'.

In 1940 and 1941 Joe privately printed two volumes of verse by herself and her girlfriend Helen Volck. The books were published under the pseudonym Hans Jacob Bernstein; in Joe's copies her own poems are marked with crosses, ticks or 'J's. It is impossible to know what Joe thought she was doing in these poems. The volumes were superficially another practical joke, with spoof forewords praising the work of 'this young Czechoslovakian refugee' and parodic dedications ('To my gifted Grandmother Natacha Lavininoff'). But the spoof, while it may excuse the clumsiness of the poetry, cannot disguise the fact it is deeply felt. The poems are raw and surprisingly passionate – if only to call Joe's bluff, it is worth taking them at face value.

The title poem of the first collection, *Smouldering Wood*, opens with the line 'I have been here before', and refers to 'the curve of memory/ Subconscious/ On a backward trend'. Having declared that she lived always in the moment, that 'I never look back', Joe portrays herself as suddenly assailed by the past. Memory, subconscious, backward: the language and the sentiments she deploys are those that would usually be horrifying to her. (In general, she took a brisk approach to psychology: 'I think some people are able to psychoanalyse themselves,' she said. 'You just tell yourself what a damn fool you are, seven times a day. Other people go to a headshrink, and pay enormous sums.')

One of her poems touches on homosexuality, another on feminism, issues which Joe rarely addressed in conversation. In *Perversities of Mankind* she notes: 'There's/ The man/ Who/ Wants/ A skirt/ And/ The girl/ Who/ Wears/ A shirt/ Even/ Fish/ That/ Want/ To fly –/ I/ Wonder why?' In *Uniform Belles*: 'no matter/ How hard/ They try/ To help/ Win the war/ And/ Clean up/ The gore/ Shouting/ Freedom and peace – /Once again/ These/ Mabels/ And Madges/ In buttons/ And badges/ Will always be/ Women/ Not/ Men!' If the political sentiments are simple, it may be because they were being tried out in Joe's mind for the first, and the last, time.

The most interesting poems concern the death of a woman. Ruth Baldwin's death seems to have raised at least one other in Joe's memory: 'I awake/ To find/ My mind/ And will have crumbled,/ The sprawling dead/ Instead/ Dwell in this stricken place.' Here is an extract from *Hotel Bedroom*:

A sigh
Of inhuman depth
Broke from the Bed.
It said,
'A week ago
Today
A broken
Battered heart
Lay
On these Pillows
And wept
Because
Her Lover
Chose another.'
Then spoke
The Desk.
'That note
She wrote
Was a suicide's farewell.'
An Armchair
In a corner
With its empty
Open arms
Spoke of her
Beauty
And her charms—
'Alas, now dead,'
The Bed said!

Just as in her life Joe reserved her deepest emotion for things, in her poetry she depicts passion as lodged with objects. Ruth did not die in a hotel room, but a hotel room was the setting for Joe's last encounter with her mother. And since both Ruth and Evelyn probably succumbed to the effects of drink or drugs, Joe might have construed both their deaths as forms of suicide, self-destructions prompted by her betrayal. In the poem *Now She's Dead*, the narrator 'finds' her love for a woman only once she has become inanimate.

> She laughed
> At other people's misery
> She drank
> Too much,
> And talked
> Incessantly.
> Her selfishness
> Was prime—
> Now
> She's dead.
>
> She lied,
> She double-crossed,
> She shamed me,
> Her tongue
> Was like a knife,
> For all the things
> She hadn't got

She blamed me—
Now
She's dead.

She teased,
She tortured all
The crumpled
Bleeding hearts
Around her door,
She kicked
And slaughtered
Many more—
Now
She's dead.

But my memory
Only sees her as a wraith
Caught in a web
Of unjust
Slander—
Standing
On her whitened pedestal
I've
Found her—
Now she's dead!

In a reversal of the Pygmalion myth, where the sculptor's love for his statue brings it to life, Joe did not find her loved ones until they died. Only inanimate objects escaped the horror of being human. Joe's poem *Impassionata* is an ode to a statue, which can be read as a tribute to the women she had loved – and to Wadley.

> Lovely vital statue
> Pure as a dream
> That has
> No bearing on reality
> No touch
> Of the human
> Horrors of tomorrow
> No time
> No place
> No afterwards––

Once dead, Ruth Baldwin escaped time, place and afterwards. Joe kept a photograph of Ruth above her bed. The picture is a close-up of Ruth's face, a fur collar and a Pekinese dog pressed up to her chin, and her dark eyes twinkling, tight with mischief and flirtation. Like twin guardians warding off the past and the future, Ruth and Wadley had pride of place in Joe's room, which she shared with none of her live lovers ('You let them sleep in the *bed* with you afterwards?' she once asked a male friend incredulously).

In her seventies Joe would see Ruth's photograph watching over her as she got out of bed and reached for her crutches.

'I look at her and she's laughing. I say, "It's all very

well for you, you're still young." She's still in her late twenties, young, adorable-looking Ruth. She says, "It doesn't really matter, it doesn't really show." '

After Ruth's death, Wadley became even more precious, his undying presence a great balm. Joe's protection of Wadley was an obsession; barely anyone was allowed to touch him, and she would not be parted from him for even a night. Whenever Joe mentioned that she was born in 1900, Wadley, she said, would ask: 'When was *that*?' If the taunting mockery of Joe's mother was transmuted in Ruth Baldwin into sweet conspiratorial laughter, her father's absence became in Wadley a perpetual innocence. Joe's father was an almost invisible figure in her life, and she made a virtue of his silence, rendered it divine by recreating it in Wadley's tacit sympathy. Nearly all the servants within the Great House on Whale Cay were male — Joe liked them for their quietness. 'They don't talk too much,' she explained. Albert Carstairs, like his daughter's next three 'fathers', wore a moustache, and there is a peculiarly melancholy photograph of Joe in early middle age, gazing at the camera with a thick dark moustache across her face.

'I like men,' Joe said. 'Most of my friends are ordinary men. I've never been frightfully fond of pansies, but manly men.'

14

~~~~~~~~~~~~

I HAD A COUNTRY GOING

Just before Christmas 1939, three months after the outbreak of the Second World War, Joe gave a banquet for 1,200 people in the southern district of Nassau. It was the first public appearance she had made in her five years in the archipelago. Joe sailed over to New Providence from Whale Cay on *Vergemere IV* with a troop of eighty boy scouts. Her 'boys' – most of them grown men – paraded through the streets, played marching tunes and then served chowder to the people. The Reverend Julian Henshaw presided over the ceremony.

Julian Henshaw, whose real name was said to be Wilfred Henshaw, was priest of the Church of Saint Catherine on Whale Cay. 'A gay priest,' said Joe, 'a very very gay priest'. The story went that Joe had shot at Henshaw, narrowly missing his head, when he first showed up unannounced on the island. In fact, Joe said, he turned up in old shorts, looking rather dirty, and she took him in. 'Go up and have a bath,' she said, 'stay the night, we'll give you food, and you must come back many times.' An educated Welshman, Henshaw claimed to have enjoyed a career as a dancer before joining the priesthood. 'The Bishop of Nassau gave him to us,' said Joe. The Bishop may well have been glad to get Henshaw off his hands.

Henshaw served as a decadent jester to Joe's court. His sermons were lively, concerning such subjects as 'Good and Bad Women of the Bible'. His church was accommodating: sometimes Fifth Day Adventists would preach there; sometimes the place would be given over to 'Jumpers' – 'They made a lot of noise and jumped around a lot,' Joe explained. Julian also taught history to the older children on the island. He was 'a great asset', said Joe: 'He did the proper thing, but he did have a few hang-ups.' At parties on Whale Cay Julian would throw open his white robes to reveal his naked body; or would take the cross from around his neck and stick it in the end of a lit cigar. He liked to take Joe's girlfriends dancing at the Jungle Club in Nassau, where he would shock the tourists by whirling around wildly, dressed in his robes and dog collar. Henshaw visited Capri with one of Joe's friends and was banished from the island after dancing on a table in a woman's nightgown. This was the kind of flamboyant mischief-making that Joe adored, for all her claims to like manly men and not 'pansies'. Henshaw was known to make sexual advances to his choirboys on Whale Cay, a practice to which Joe for a time turned a blind eye. He described the island as 'Utopia'.

Henshaw drank heavily, and tried to charge his alcohol bills to Joe; on one occasion this elicited a playful but irritated reprimand from Alfred Agostini, the island treasurer. In a letter addressed to 'The Not Too Reverend Henshaw' at 'St Catherine's Rectory, The Midlands, Whale Cay', Agostini wrote: 'In fact and in a word, I am *certain* that Miss Carstairs would desire me to tell you to pay your own damn liquor bills and not keep having them sent to this office month after month in the (I can assure you, futile) hope that they will slip past the eagle eye of the Chancellor and, in the mad shuffle of pounds and ten, somehow get paid at no expense to your reverend self . . .' The letter was signed 'alfred agostini, gentleman in ordinary to M. B. Carstairs'. Henshaw replied to 'The Chancellor Agostini', pleading to 'invoke your august and venerable clemency, forebearance and longsuffering with those responsible for the document which has caused your office so much concern for they live in a world which knows not what it does'.

Those who worked with Joe joined in the fantasy that Whale Cay was a kingdom, with an omnipotent ruler, a stern chancellor, a corrupt church, a well-drilled army, an ocean-going fleet, a flourishing

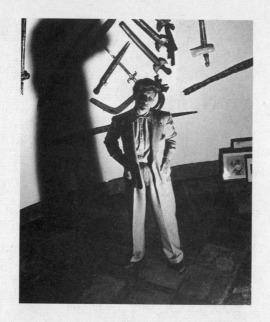

Joe Carstairs in the Museum at Whale Cay

The Great House at Whale Cay, completed in 1936

Charlotte, who lived on Whale Cay with Joe
in the 1940s

Jorie, who lived on Whale Cay with Joe in
the late 1950s

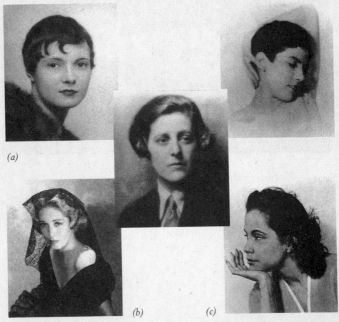

A few of the 120 pictures of girlfriends in Joe's collection, including Mabs Jenkins *(a)*, Helen Volck *(b)*, Blanche Dunn *(c)*, Gwen Farrar *(d)* and Teddie Gerard *(e)*

Joe Carstairs with Jackki at a fishing tournament
in the 1950s

The Reverend Julian Henshaw, priest on Whale Cay

Joe with Jackki in the 1980s

Wadley in the 1970s

'Narcissus', a portrait of Wadley in the 1920s

economy and obedient subjects. 'I had a country going,' said Joe. 'I ran a country.'

Joe issued scores of admonitory notices. 'Notice,' read one. 'I eat brown rice in preference to white. Therefore, if brown rice is good enough for me and my household, it is good enough or even too good for the people. M. B. Carstairs.'

'The strictest law of Whale Cay', ran a notice of 1940, 'is that no alcoholic liquor may be drunk or be in the possession of any person while under my jurisdiction. The continual breaking of this law has caused me to stop all Andros leave until the August holidays. Those wishing to go to Andros will do so at the risk of not being permitted to return to this island. There will *not* be a holiday on Good Friday. It is unfortunate that the innocent have to be punished with the guilty.'

Several signs took the form of warnings: 'All bicycles ridden at night must be equipped with a proper light. Anyone found riding his bicycle at night without a light, will have his bicycle taken from him.' And in 1941:

NOTICE

THERE ARE CERTAIN PEOPLE ON THIS JOB
WHO MAY BE FIRED AT ANY <u>MOMENT</u>——
THEY ARE <u>SLOW</u>, <u>LAZY</u> AND **<u>UNSATISFACTORY</u>**

THE FOLLOWING SHOULD <u>BEWARE</u>.

JOE BRENNEN	TARAH BROWN
ROLAND MILLER	JAY MINNIS
<u>GEORGE FERGUSON</u>	HILGROVE LIGHTBOURNE
HERMAN BAIN	WILFRED PHINE
ZEPHENIAH DEAN	

THERE ARE OTHERS WHO ARE ALSO IN THE

<u>**FIRING LINE . . .**</u>

To this Joe added, in handwriting: 'If this kind of thing happens again <u>every man</u> on the job will be made to suffer. MBC.'

'Make something of yourselves,' Joe enjoined in speeches to her people. 'Quit this ridiculous drinking and marauding.'

Joe was at pains to point out that she was not running a charity. Asked if she would raise wages if Whale Cay turned a profit, she replied: 'God, no. That would be philanthropy. I detest the word. I'm the fellow with the hand in his pocket.'

The Whale Cay economy was circular and self-contained: the money Joe paid in wages was spent at the store and so returned to her coffers to be paid out again. The islanders were encouraged to use a community bank but they tended to carry their wages in their shoes or handkerchiefs, and when the notes became too dirty in this endless round Joe exchanged them for clean cash in Nassau. The Whale Cay store, by 1940 the biggest in the Bahamas, stocked clothes, blankets, meats (from corned beef to roast mutton), tobacco, Quaker Oats, Coca-Cola, buttons, chocolate. Beer and wine were available, but strictly rationed. Joe filled the shop with supplies she bought at wholesale prices in Nassau and which she sold at cost. On trips to the capital she also visited the Old England Stores, where she would buy a few yards of doeskin or tweed to have made into suits for herself, her girlfriends and Wadley.

Those who lived on Whale Cay remembered Joe Carstairs with respect and affection. They were like her own children, they said. Joe sacked white managers who worked the blacks too hard. She insisted that the islanders go to church every Sunday and that they contribute to a health-care fund, which insured them against hospital treatment. To prevent the spread of disease Joe at one point forbade travel between islands. In Nassau she donated a substantial sum to the Bahamas General Hospital, with which it established the Carstairs ward for children, and she helped found a grammar school. Joe paid for and arranged the funeral of anyone who died on Whale Cay. And, as long as they behaved, Joe allowed her islanders some fun. At Christmas she provided fifty-five-gallon drums of wine; she laid on splendid wedding parties; and the weekly dances at the store were renowned throughout the Out Islands.

Children born on Whale Cay were usually taken to Joe to be named, a tradition that stemmed from the days of the slave plantation. She dubbed the first boy Samuel Octagon Brennan: the Samuel may have been for Samuel Saunders, who built Joe's first boat; Octagon was the brand of soap stocked in the island store. For several of the girls she chose the names she had spurned, Marion Barbara. 'God knows why,' Joe remarked.

A day school was provided for the island children and a night school for the adults, 90 per cent of whom were illiterate. On the schoolroom wall hung a sign reading 'Long Live the King'. Joe's boy scout troop, the 87th Bahamas, was in effect a private army of almost 100 men. To teach her soldiers to drill, Joe showed them a film of the guards parading at Buckingham Palace and instructed them to copy their moves exactly. During exercises the troops sometimes flinched and scratched as they were bitten by mosquitoes. Joe admonished them: 'Look here. You're not to stir even if a Bengal tiger snaps at your ankles. Get it?' According to Joe, mosquitoes did not bite her because they could tell she was not afraid of them.

In 1940, the Duke of Windsor was made Governor of the Bahamas in an attempt by the British government to shuffle him and the Duchess off the international stage for the duration of the war. As Edward VIII, he had been dethroned and exiled for offending propriety, much as Joe Carstairs, Speed Queen, had been before him. The Duke of Windsor and his divorcee wife became mock-monarchs in a distant and irrelevant colony; Joe did rather better, creating her own monarchy in the Bahamas as the White Queen of Whale Cay.

When the Windsors arrived in Nassau the 87th Bahamas, Joe's soldier-boys, were among the troops lining the streets: they bore nickel-plated staves and were beautifully turned out, their limbs shining with oil. The new Governor and his wife were regaled with music by a band of twenty-five Whale Cay boys.

In January 1941 the Duke and Duchess paid a visit to Whale Cay, and *Life* magazine took photographs of their progress round the island. 'Damn it,' said the Duke of Windsor as he inspected the roads, 'why can't all the Out Islands make roads like these?' Joe showed them her boats in the dock, and while the Duke was on the deck of one of the yachts she took the Duchess into the cabin. The Duchess saw Wadley. 'Who is *that*?' she asked (Joe was impressed that she said 'who' rather than 'what'). Joe introduced her: 'That's my boy, that's Wadley.' 'My God,' said the Duchess, 'he's just like my husband.'

Joe found the Duke boring and morose but she lent him public support. 'Fortunately we have a Governor whose heart beats in the soil,' she wrote in a letter to the *Nassau Tribune*. As for the Duchess, 'She was a marvellous person. The English didn't like her but I thought she was great.' Julian Henshaw also befriended the Windsors, and spread scurrilous gossip about them (he claimed to have it on the authority of one of the Windsors' servants that the Duke was far from well-endowed).

Soon *Life* and the *Saturday Evening Post* ran cover stories trumpeting Joe Carstairs's achievements. For the Bahamas Fair in Nassau that February, Joe wrote a manifesto describing her aims on Whale Cay. 'It is with the hope in mind that the Bahamas will one day be sufficient unto themselves that this project has been undertaken . . . The ambition is to train the people to be expert workers in their various trades which includes: Cabinet making, carpentry, shipbuilding, masonry, farming, engineering, book-keeping, Domestic service, and (last but not least) to teach them to live in cleanliness and order so that they and the generations of the future, shall be fitted to make a decent livelihood, and to be an asset rather than a liability to the community.'

In the Whale Cay booth at the fair she presented garden peas and celery grown on the island, asparagus, beets, carrots, cucumbers, citrus fruit, bananas and canteloupes. She displayed a hutch of rabbits – 'the ideal poor man's food' – and the Whale Cay flag, a yellow sunburst on blue cloth. But the central exhibit was a scale model of the island, constructed at a cost of about $3,000 with the help of her friend Bart Howard. The miniature church was lit from within so that its stained-glass windows shone out. When the church bells rang the lighthouse beacon flashed. It was, in a sense, a Whale Cay for Wadley – the perfection of Joe's endeavours.

In March the film director Gabriel Pascal premièred his *Major Barbara* in Nassau, in honour of the Windsors. He too visited Whale Cay. 'With the possible exception of Katie Hepburn,' he said, 'Miss Carstairs is the cleverest woman I ever met. I'd like to have her in my next picture.' Joe would have been flattered by this comparison: she thought her voice was like Katharine Hepburn's and said that if a film were made of her life, Hepburn should play the lead.

The number of natives on Whale Cay – which stood at 150 in 1939 and 250 in 1940 – now swelled to 500. It was a measure of the economic importance of Joe's settlement that she spent more than $250,000 on the construction of her island and paid out $1,200 a week in wages, while the Bahamas as a whole exported only $700,000-worth of produce a year.

'People are so desperately in need of work,' Joe told the *The Tribune* in 1941, 'that they take any risk in reaching my island. Twelve people left Andros to come to Whale Cay the other day but only three reached it –

the other nine were drowned. Some of these belonged to families of my people.' In 1941, for the first time, Whale Cay made some money, by selling vegetables to a cannery which provided tinned food for soldiers. In June *The Herald*, a liberal Bahamian newspaper, described Joe's achievement as 'the greatest story since the landing of Christopher Columbus in this colony'.

15

JOIN HANDS ON THE
ROADWAY TO THE SUN

'I wanted to elevate the standard of living for the black people,' Joe said. 'I knew damn well that I had the answer.'

In 1939 Joe Carstairs set up an organisation 'to bring Properity to the Coloured People of the Bahamas'. She named it the Coloured League of Youth, not because it was open only to the young but because it was designed to rejuvenate a whole race. 'The rest of the world has a bad opinion of the Coloured People of these Islands,' noted the manifesto. 'The Coloured People do not prosper in the way they should. They do not seem to care, or want to get on. THIS MUST BE CHANGED.'

The league was at once an altruistic project and a bid by Joe to extend her empire, to defy the white ruling class in Nassau and become the *de facto* ruler of the British West Indies. The success of Joe's settlement on Whale Cay had convinced her that she had the key to revitalising the entire colony, and she was now trying to initiate a social and economic revolution in the Bahamas. She more than once voiced the opinion that she ought to be made governor. 'Everybody would have followed me,' she said.

'Be clever,' urged Joe's manifesto for the Coloured League of Youth, 'believe in yourselves, be moral, sober, clean and healthy. Fill yourselves with the spirit of progress, have the wish to succeed – join hands on the Roadway to the Sun.'

Despite the Utopian rhetoric, Joe's plans were firmly rooted in local politics and economics. Ever since the emancipation of Bahamian slaves a century earlier, attempts to make the archipelago agriculturally viable had failed. In part, this was because the Out Islands were widely scattered and resistant to cultivation; but Joe was convinced that if the people organised transport and the distribution of fertiliser, these problems could be overcome. She was also up against the white politicians in Nassau, known as the 'Bay Street Boys' because they owned the businesses in the town's main street. These merchants made their money through imports, and had no interest in promoting native agriculture. They controlled the boats that travelled between islands and set the prices in Nassau shops. Joe planned to challenge their power.

Joe was Chief Comptroller of the league, and beneath her was an elaborate hierarchy of comptrollers for propaganda, agriculture, accounts and public works, as well as medical, legal and religious officers (the Reverend Julian Henshaw filled this last post). Those who wanted to join the league nominated themselves to an officer, and if approved attended an initiation ceremony. There the nominee repeated a series of prayers, oaths and promises, which were punctuated with drum-rolls and bugle-blasts. At the end a badge was pinned to the new member. According to the constitution, 'The Member is then handed his Membership card and takes his leave in silence. As the Member passes out of the building, or meeting-place, a bugle-call shall be sounded, so that those outside shall know another Member has been made.' Joe, believing in her own repeated rebirths, was trying to recreate the black populace, one by one.

Members of the league were entitled to apply to farm on Bird Cay, a small island two miles from Whale Cay, or on their own islands. For the first year the league (that is, Joe) would supply the farmers with free food, clothes, a ration of beer and cigarettes, seeds, tools, fertilisers and advice on farming techniques. Members would be paid no wages, and instead would receive a voucher to the value of the produce they brought to a central market. After a year the free supplies and subsistence would be withdrawn and the farmers would be allowed to sell their fruit and vegetables for money.

Joe further proposed that members of the CLY open a store in Nassau to sell only local produce and compete with the imported fruit and vegetables that were for sale in the rest of the town. She suggested that the league purchase a freight boat to transport Out Island goods to the capital, and hire an agricultural expert to advise on farming techniques. She guaranteed all members of the league free medical treatment, legal and religious advice; in special cases, extra money could be provided for the construction of greenhouses and rain tanks. The goal was self-sufficiency. Just as in her private life Joe strove to need nothing and no one (Wadley excepted), in her public projects she preached self-reliance and independence above all else.

Joe had black girlfriends, though none of them was Bahamian. In about 1940 she had an affair with the beautiful Blanche Dunn, who after a small role in *The Emperor Jones* (1933) had retired from acting to pursue a series of glamorous and often scandalous liaisons; one of her lovers was killed by his jealous wife, and Blanche herself once went after Joe with a carving knife, causing her to leap out of a hotel window. Joe also had platonic friendships with black women. In France in the 1930s she met the singer Mabel Mercer, who by the end of the decade 'had become my sister almost'. 'I thought she was a very great lady and had a marvellous voice,' said Joe. 'She was very proper, you know, just the opposite to me.' Afraid that the Nazis would persecute Mabel because of her colour, Joe urged her to leave Paris before war broke out. Mabel Mercer crossed the Atlantic to America in 1938 – Joe paid her passage – and she became a regular visitor to Whale Cay. She had a 'green thumb', Joe said, and planted trees all over the island. Mabel went on to form a musical partnership with the composer Bart Howard, of whom Joe was also a friend and patron, and recorded his composition *Fly Me To The Moon* before it was popularised by Peggy Lee.

On Whale Cay in the 1930s and 1940s, Joe employed blacks as well as whites as store managers, teachers, clergy, and so on, while in Nassau job segregation persisted into the 1960s. When dining with a black friend in a restaurant in the still segregated American South, Joe was approached by a disapproving waitress. 'Is this lady coloured?' the woman asked. 'Certainly not!' roared Joe, countering one absurdity with another. She was something of a hero to the liberal Bahamian newspaper *The Herald* for her outspoken championing of black self-improvement. And at one level the Coloured League of Youth was a pioneering body for the economic emancipation of Bahamian blacks. The manifesto stated that the Bahamas were run by and for whites, and that it was up to the blacks to change this.

Joe too felt thwarted by the establishment – first in Britain, now in Nassau. She identified with the blacks as brothers in exile, plain working people up against the forces of convention and entrenched power. But to her the blacks were subjects as well as comrades, and her feelings about them were a peculiar jumble of idealism and prejudice. In her rebellion Joe had effectively modelled herself on a colonial ruler. The persona she constructed drew on old-fashioned models of manhood: she stood for Empire, Britishness, cleanliness, hard work, physical bravery, moral fibre. The Coloured League of Youth was correspondingly paternalistic, run principally by whites and predicated on weaknesses in the black race.

'It is not only their colour which has prevented and hindered them, and left so many in abject poverty,' Joe wrote in the manifesto. 'It is because so many of them are foolish, and not to be trusted, or relied upon. A people, most of them, who know not Truth, or Morals. They have not intelligence; nor do they see that they have a responsibility towards the great Empire to which they belong – and to this land in which they were born.'

Despite this rather strong proviso, the white merchants in Nassau were convinced that the league was dangerously subversive. The Bay Street Boys, who occupied most of the seats in the House of Assembly, warned Joe that her organisation could incite racial hatred, and demanded that she close it. In 1940 Joe withdrew the original CLY manifesto and issued a new circular stating that 'the movement does not seek to create animosity between the two races but merely tries to help the coloured race to advance economically and socially'. Though it was true that the Bahamas were run for whites, Joe wrote, this was 'fair and right'. 'These islands were discovered by White People, founded by White People, governed by White People . . . And apart from a few who have proven their ability, around them and behind them throng a rabble of Coloured folk, waiting for crumbs to drop from their tables.' Members of the league were told that they should acknowledge 'For the present we must be led' and admit 'It is *our* fault. We have been sleepy and stupid.'

The Bay Street Boys were temporarily appeased but towards the end of 1941 Joe launched a direct attack on the government of the British West Indies, blaming it for both the poverty of the people and the high incidence of syphilis in the colony.

'Whenever my Negroes go to Nassau,' Carstairs complained to the *New York World Telegram*, 'they come back infected with syphilis. The tourists are kept in ignorance of these conditions. They see only the picturesque . . . The Bahamian House of Assembly is to blame for these conditions. It is the parliament of Nassau. Its members are the merchants of Bay

Street. All they care about is the tourist trade. It's a damn shame, a disgrace. The health and economic status of their people means absolutely nothing to the House of Assembly crowd. The islands should be worked on an agricultural basis. I've proved that any vegetable in the world can be grown in the Bahamas . . . The merchants of Bay St would rather import alligator pears and sell them at 75 cents apiece than buy native-grown ones which could sell at a few cents each. Why? Because there is more profit in big prices.'

The House of Assembly was incensed. Joe Carstairs was an 'ungracious guest', its members raged, who had 'been given refuge in this colony from features she did not like about her own country' and was now 'slandering the good name of these islands'. The newspaper interview she had given caused the biggest sensation in the Bahamas since the announcement that the Duke of Windsor was to be appointed Governor. The government discussed the possibility of hauling Joe before the Bar of the House or of deporting her. She had overstepped the mark.

By the end of 1941 Joe had been spurned on all sides. The Coloured League of Youth, now shorn of its fighting spirit, faded to nothing. When the United States entered the war in 1941 many Bahamians moved to America to fill the farm and factory jobs that had fallen empty. At the same time the philanthropist multi-millionaire Sir Harry Oakes funded the construction of two airfields on New Providence, a project which provided well-paid work for thousands of Bahamians. Some of Joe's islanders started to leave her.

Joe tried to do her bit for the war effort. When the British Navy issued a request for boats to be handed over for use as minesweepers, she immediately offered *Sonia II*. 'This ship,' Joe wrote in a press release, 'one of the most beautiful private schooners in the world, has been placed by Miss Carstairs unreservedly at the service of His Majesty's Navy.' His Majesty's Navy turned *Sonia II* down as unsuitable. When the Japanese bombed Pearl Harbor, Joe offered the ship to the American Navy and again it was refused.

She presented the Duke of Windsor with a plan to establish fighting and farming task forces which would make the colony self-sufficient during the war. He ignored it.

Joe, of course, longed to see service in the war herself. She asked the advice of her half-brother, Francis Francis, on how to enlist. He hit her where it hurt. 'Wrong age,' said Frank, 'wrong sex.'

16

~~~~~~~~

THE NEVERLAND

'I don't know if you have ever seen a map of a person's mind,' wrote J. M. Barrie in *Peter Pan*:

Doctors sometimes draw maps of other parts of you, and your own map can become intensely interesting, but catch them trying to draw a map of a child's mind, which is not only confused, but keeps going round all the time. There are zigzag lines on it, just like your temperature on a card, and there are probably roads on the island; for the Neverland is always more or less an island, with astonishing splashes of colour here and there, and coral reefs and rakish-looking craft in the offing, and savages and lonely lairs, and gnomes who are mostly tailors, and caves through which a river runs, and princes with six elder brothers, and a hut fast going to decay, and one very small old lady with a hooked nose. It would be an easy map if that were all, but there is also the first day at school, religion, fathers, the round pond, needlework, murders, hangings, verbs that take the dative, chocolate-pudding day, getting into braces, say ninety-nine, threepence for pulling out your tooth yourself, and so on; and either these are part of the island or they are another map showing through, and it is all rather confusing, especially as nothing will ever stand still . . . On these magic shores children at play are forever beaching their coracles. We too have been there; we can still hear the sound of the surf, though we shall land no more.

Joe Carstairs did land again on the Neverland. As Wadley was an image of her soul, Whale Cay was its map. The island, Joe believed, was her own creation: 'I didn't make *improvements*,' she pointed out impatiently. 'There was nothing there. I made just what I wanted.' By inventing a counter-kingdom, a fantasy world in which to live, she defied the censures and strictures of the adult world. In 1941 she was shunned once again by that world, and once again she retreated to her Neverland. Whale Cay was a region of her self, and so it had no chronology. Here she could be a boy who never had to grow up.

In her teenage years Joe had experienced a recurrent dream which she later interpreted as a premonition, a vision of Whale Cay. It can also be read as a reliving of her momentous crossing to America in 1911, in which she 'left family aged 11'.

In the dream she would find herself aboard a small steamship, crowded with baggage and people, sailing in beautiful blue sea. The sky too was very blue, dotted with clouds, and a high wind was blowing. Then land came into view, a shore of sand dunes laden with tall jungle grass blowing in the breeze; the dunes were a creamy pink, and the grass the colour of wheat. On one of the dunes was a building shaped like the Flatiron Building in New York. Joe longed to leave the ship for the land – which was strange, she remarked, because she usually longed to be on ships. But she could not disembark because she was unable to find her baggage among that of all the other people. 'If I could only get off this boat,' she thought, 'but I've got to have my luggage.'

'This dream was always the same,' Joe said, 'and I never did get off the boat. Exactly the same, as if it was stamped.'

In her early thirties Joe Carstairs finally stepped on to her island, leaving her baggage behind her. By buying Whale Cay she expelled for ever the dream she had carried. On the island she was able to live out her fantasies, externalise all that was inside her, so that she remained untroubled by emotion and memory.

The Darlings, too, know the Neverland when they reach it: 'Strange to say, they all recognized it at once.' Just as Whale Cay called to Joe, the Neverland beckons the Darling children in *Peter Pan*: 'The island was looking out for them. It is only thus that anyone may sight those magic shores.' And where Whale Cay was roused by Joe, the Neverland is roused by Peter Pan. 'Feeling that Peter was on his way back, the Neverland had again woke into life . . . With the coming of Peter, who hates lethargy, they are all under way again: if you put your ear to the ground now, you would hear the whole island seething with life.'

To Joe, lethargy was death. She was once asked whether she missed racing boats after buying Whale Cay. 'You can't qualify movement,' she replied. 'It's a different kind of speed.' The island was a place where you lived for ever because nothing stood still. It was so vibrant that Joe barely slept. 'Some people', she observed, 'sleep a very dead sleep. I don't. I sleep lightly, wake up two or three times. I sleep on the top of the bed.' As if the bed might prove a grave, she lay on it rather than in it; as if sleep were death, she refused to enter it too deeply. 'I've really kept awfully young by the way I've lived,' she said. 'I live young.' She had come to Whale Cay in the same spirit as the Spanish explorer Ponce de Leon had come to the Bahamas in 1513, seeking a fountain of everlasting youth. He claimed to have found it on the Bimini Islands, twenty miles or so west of Whale Cay.

Movement to Joe was a defiance of death, a way

of outrunning mortality. She seemed to feel she could beat death by denying it, that she could devour her time and so escape being devoured by it. Friends remarked that they did not once hear Joe say that she was tired. The emblem of Whale Cay was a sun, an image of perpetual day; the island flag was hoisted daily alongside the Union Jack. The little god of Whale Cay was Wadley, unageing, unchangeable and still. Like the island, he carried the weight of Joe's desire, leaving her to travel light.

Joe stayed young by forgetting the past, and with it the future. 'No one ever gets over the first unfairness,' writes Barrie, 'no one except Peter. He often met it, but he always forgot it. I suppose that was the real difference between him and the rest.' It was Joe's gift, too, immediately to forget wrongs done her. 'Can you remember anyone who ever did you dirt?' asked a friend. 'No,' Carstairs replied. 'No. If they did I would have cast it out.'

As well as sanitising her past, she cast out dirt – the signs of mortality and decay – in the houses of Whale Cay. Joe organised a collection service for rubbish, which was burnt at designated sites on the island. She inspected the islanders' huts for cleanliness every month. The men who lived alone, Joe noticed, were cleaner than those who shared a house with a wife.

The Great House, white within and without, was regularly repainted. Each bedroom was equipped with a huge bathroom. Ostensibly for fear of contracting syphilis, Joe never sat on lavatory seats but always stood. Downstairs the chairs were backed with vinyl, for easy cleaning, or with white leather, and the floor was laid with gleaming lobster-back-pink tiles. One man was employed solely to polish the silver, another to polish the copper and brass lamps. Bertram, the half-Syrian, half-Bahamian butler, waited at table in white gloves. The sturdy, ample furniture was made on the island of native wood – mahogany, lignum vitae. The kitchen was big, with stainless steel cabinets and linoleum.

Four women ran the laundry, working day and night; the quality of their washing was so celebrated that visitors to the island would bring with them suitcases of dirty clothes. 'If one went to the bathroom and took off a shirt,' a friend remembered, 'three or four black women would come and grab it and take it to the laundry room.' Joe changed her shirt two or three times a day and ordered forty new shirts at a time from her tailor. She insisted that her white shirts be washed by the best laundress, Miss Martha, and put out in the sun to dry. She was delighted when a friend's mother described her as 'clean-cut'.

Though she liked to play the doctor and to cure illness, Joe could not bear to be in the company of those who were sick. Guests with colds were encouraged to stay in their rooms. In the late 1940s the Reverend Julian Henshaw went with one of Joe's girlfriends on a trip to Rome, where he was rumoured to have conducted a Black Mass. When Henshaw returned it emerged that he had contracted syphilis. Joe was horrified: 'How can you sleep with all those boys and be a priest?' she demanded. She threw Henshaw off the island. His condition deteriorated and he shortly afterwards died in a Nassau hospital. Joe said Henshaw's spirit would career around the world paying penance for his sins. 'There's no rest for Julian,' she said. 'He goes round and round.'

Joe had been impelled to action by Henshaw's physical sickness, but she was clearly upset by his moral degeneracy, especially since it involved the corruption of youth. Joe loved little boys as equals – they were at their best, she said, between the ages of seven and fifteen. 'They think of me as one of them . . . they like me like another little boy.' One boy on Whale Cay, she recalled, had told her conspiratorially that his father was an old person – the father was in his forties at the time, younger than Joe. This showed, she claimed, that the boy 'was not conscious of any age group as far as I was concerned'. The children on Whale Cay called Joe 'my relative'.

The first white child to be born on Whale Cay was a girl, Blanche Lowe, the daughter of the captain of Joe's boats. Hutchins Lowe was an orphan who had run away to sea at sixteen; before Joe employed him, he had been running rum as well as mail and food. Joe, perhaps disappointed that her captain's first-born was not a boy, dressed Blanche in khaki like a tiny soldier. Blanche and her younger sisters grew up as tomboys, shooting marbles, playing ball, running wild in the bush, in the care of an old black man named Jake. 'After Daddy produced four girls,' reflected one of Blanche's sisters, 'I guess Miss Carstairs kind of gave up on him.' But Joe retained a great fondness for Blanche, and when the child developed a tumour on her leg sent her to New York for treatment.

Joe also took under her wing Ben Dawkins, a black boy, giving him work in the Great House, smart clothes, an education. She encouraged him to train as a boxer but was angry when he left the island as a young man to try his luck in Florida – the trouble with real boys was that they grew into men, and went away. When Ben Dawkins told Joe that he planned to enter boxing matches as 'The Whale', in honour of Whale Cay, Joe relented a little and had some robes made for him.

In the early 1950s the Reverend Prince Hepburn, a garrulous and charming black priest from one of the poorer sections of Nassau, approached Joe with a request to hold a summer camp for underprivileged boys on Whale Cay. Joe agreed and offered to provide transport, accommodation and food. Hepburn thanked her, but said he would organise the food – they must do something for themselves. 'Well, by damn,' said Joe. 'I meet the first Bahamian who doesn't request the horse and the saddle too.' She jumped up from her chair and shook his hand. 'Congratulations. I go for you.' The camp took up residence on the island each summer for the rest of Joe's time there. 'I find Joe Carstair to be very kind but also very demanding,' reported Prince Hepburn. 'Ms Carstair was a disciplinary. She could be very mean at times. When that steam was over she was calm, forgiving and meek.' Joe loved to visit her colony of lost boys. These boys, conveniently, always left the island before they grew up. Sometimes when Joe visited Nassau in later years, men would stop her in the street and say, 'I was one of your boys at Whale Cay.' A girls' camp was also established on the island, but Joe showed no interest in it.

On Whale Cay, Joe sought not to turn boys into men but men – and women and girls – into boys. She was always surrounded by 'little people, little boys', a friend recalled. For all her sexual exploits, Joe seemed to hanker after a sexless, pre-pubescent kingdom. In her fantasy land, there was no breeding, only self-invention. Joe expressed her horror of pro-creation in *Living Death*, one of the poems from her first volume:

The lustful lungings of the masses,
Trundling home perambulators,
Striving to increase the nation—
Indiscriminate copulators.

When Joe gave out the wages at the store on a Friday
she would make a speech to the workers. Sometimes
in this speech she complained that there were too
many babies being born on the island – 'Keep it in
your pants,' she suggested.

As Joe saw it, sex not only bred children but also
betrayal. She proved this in her own life by repeatedly
cheating on her lovers, as her mother had before her.
'I'm much more loyal to friends than I am to the other
kind,' Joe said. Lord Tod Wadley was her ideal: he
was a little man who had no genitals and he was a
child immaculately conceived: a motherless boy.

Mothers are anathema to the Neverland. When at
the end of *Peter Pan* Peter visits the grown-up Wendy,
now a mother herself, she feels 'helpless and guilty,
a big woman'. 'Hallo, Wendy,' says Peter. '"Hallo,
Peter," she replied faintly, squeezing herself as small
as possible. Something inside her was crying, "Woman,
woman, let go of me."' Joe's desire to always be fit
and trim was a desire to ward off womanliness, to
preserve the body of a boy and so earn eternal
admittance to the Neverland. 'Joe has *breasts?*' the
son of a friend asked with mock-incredulity when

she was in her eighties. 'That's difficult for me to think about.'

The erasure of adulthood carried cruelty with it. The Neverland, Barrie notes, will last for as long as children are 'gay and innocent and heartless'. Joe's games and practical jokes were laced with spite. She would make gratuitous assertions of her power. One friend remembered that during a fishing trip Joe spotted a stingray, and insisted that everyone jump in the water. In *Peter Pan* the Lost Boys are not allowed to speak of their mothers in Peter's presence, and 'When they seem to be growing up, which is against the rules, Peter thins them out.' If people did not play by Joe's rules on the island, she threw them off.

This cruelty came into being, though, to stave off grief. Peter Pan, like Joe Carstairs, presents his exile on the Neverland as a wilful escape: 'I ran away the day I was born.' But towards the end of the book he reveals that he once flew back to his mother, only to find the window shut and another boy in his bed. Mothers, he decided, were 'very overrated persons'. When the Darlings and the Lost Boys, ignoring his warnings about mothers, decide to leave the Neverland, Peter 'cared very much; and he was so full of wrath against grown-ups, who as usual were spoiling everything, that as soon as he got inside his tree he breathed intentionally quick short breaths at the rate of about five to a second. He did this because there is a saying in the Neverland that every time you breathe, a grown-up dies; and Peter was killing them off as vindictively as possible.'

The sadness and cruelty of the Neverland surfaces in a poem Joe wrote in 1941. It concerns Wadley's genesis in the Swiss mountain stall from which Ruth Baldwin had bought him in 1925, and it casts Wadley as a Lost Boy:

> He stood upon a snowclad wall
> The tiny mountain guide
> A little bent old woman
> Sat knitting by his side
>
> With all her wares around her
> The stall was very neat
> At Rosegg in the Engadine—
> Upon a mountain peak
>
> Her customers were many
> The season in full swing
> Beyond the hills and mountain rills
> The churchbells softly ring
>
> But there's sadness to my story
> As often is the case
> The shining little mountain guide
> Was stolen from his place

> The little bent old woman
> Had loved him as her son
> Even though he was a toy-child
> He was the 'only one'!

In Joe's poem Wadley is stolen from his foster mother, transported like Peter's companions to a motherless land. Joe stored her memories in Wadley instead of herself, and this poem must carry the memory of a scene from her own past. Perhaps Joe is remembering the nanny she loved, from whom she was taken. Or maybe she is imagining that before the birth of her siblings she was, though just a girl-child, still her mother's 'only one' — and that she was loved then as if she were a son.

17

<center>~~~~~~~~~</center>

I DON'T GIVE A FUCK
ABOUT THE LAW

S ometimes – and this was the joy of having a
doll with which to play – Wadley could be
the angel to Joe's devil, the spotless sailor
boy to her pirate, Peter Pan to her Captain
Hook. From the moment she reached Whale Cay, Joe
was an outlaw as well as a lawmaker.

In the early eighteenth century, the Bahamas was
an anarchic Pirates' Republic. More than a thousand
pirates roamed the archipelago, plundering ships and
taking refuge on the islands from the law and from
storms. On the tiny cays they buried their treasure,
repaired their boats in the harbours and creeks, set
up their ships' guns on the shore and whiled away
the hours – like Joe – with games and skits. The men
would entertain themselves by staging mock trials and
executions.

Joe had sailed to Cocos Island in search of buried
treasure in 1931, and on Whale Cay she hoped to
unearth chests of gold. She did find some evidence

that the island had been a pirates' lair: there were cannon balls in the waterholes, and she turned up an old Spanish knife, which she added to the collection in the museum.

The most famous of the eighteenth-century buccaneers was Edward Teach, or Blackbeard, who in *Peter Pan* is described as the man whom Hook served as bosun before becoming a captain himself. Almost as celebrated in the Bahamas were the pirates Mary Read and Anne Bonny. These female buccaneers defied the laws of the land and the superstitions of the sea: traditionally, having a woman on board a ship brought bad luck. 'They wore Men's Jackets,' wrote Captain Charles Johnson in his eighteenth-century history of the pirates, 'and long Trouzers, and Handkerchiefs tied about their Heads . . . each of them had a Machet and Pistol in their Hands and cursed and Swore at the Men.' When the two were captured and threatened with death, Mary Read said she approved of the punishment: if it were not for hanging, she reasoned, cowards would turn to piracy and deprive the truly courageous of their spoils.

Anne Bonny's captain and lover, Jack Rackham, was something of a dandy, known as 'Calico Jack' because of his penchant for bright waistcoats, ribbons and breeches. In *Peter Pan*, J. M. Barrie notes that the 'dark nature' of Captain Hook was run through with 'a touch of the feminine, as in all great pirates'. Pirates inhabited and exploited the fringes of society, and this translated readily into sexual ambiguity. The confusions of gender in the Bahamian pirate myths were such that at one point, it was said, Mary Read joined Rackham's ship disguised as a sailor and Anne Bonny, mistaking her for a man, tried to seduce her.

Marlene Dietrich, who herself made a career out of sexual ambiguity, knew Joe Carstairs as 'The Pirate'. The two met in the summer of 1937 in the South of France; every year Joe gave her workers a holiday in the months of July and August and took herself off to the United States or Europe. At first Joe studiously ignored Marlene, who reproached her for this when they were introduced – 'Why didn't you look at me?' 'Because you were Dietrich,' Joe replied. They met again in 1938 and together bought a boat named *Arkel*.

In the summer of 1939 Joe sailed a schooner from Whale Cay to the Cap d'Antibes to see Dietrich. An account of the meeting between the two is given by Dietrich's daughter, Maria Riva, in her biography of her mother. Dietrich was on holiday in the South of France with her lover (the novelist Erich Remarque), her daughter, her husband and his mistress.

One day, everyone was 'a-twitter'. They congregated along the rocks like hungry sea gulls, searching the surface of the sea. A strange ship had been sighted making for our private cove. A magnificent, three-masted schooner, its black hull skimming through the glassy water, its teak decks gleaming in the morning sun, at the helm, a beautiful boy. Bronzed and sleek – even from a distance, one sensed the power of the rippling muscles of his tight chest and haunches. He waved at his appreciative audience, flashed a rakish white-toothed smile, and gave the command to drop anchor among the white yachts. If he had run up the Jolly Roger, no one would have been surprised. The first thought on seeing him had been Pirate – followed by Pillage and Plunder.

My mother touched Remarque's arm. 'Boni – isn't he beautiful? He must be coming here for lunch. Who is he?' She watched him being rowed ashore. Dressed in skin-tight ducks and striped sailor's jersey, he climbed the steps leading up to the Eden Roc and turned from a sexy boy into a sexy, flat-chested woman.

(When Joe ran into Greta Garbo at a New York optician's, this sexually ambiguous screen icon, too, mistook her for a man. 'Hello, Miss Garbo,' Joe said. 'Hello, sir,' Garbo replied.)

While the Dietrich family dubbed Joe 'the Pirate', Joe, Maria noted, 'was the only one who ever called Dietrich "Babe" and got away with it'; her other nicknames for Dietrich were 'Mother' and 'Doctor' (the latter derived from her initials, M.D.). Throughout the summer Maria would help to dress her mother for daily rendezvous on Carstairs's ship, *Sonia II*. These meetings were kept secret from Remarque – Joe and Marlene enjoyed a heady, clandestine affair.

Joe was dark, tough and compact where Dietrich was fair and willowy; and Joe's reclusive exile counterpointed Dietrich's extraordinary fame. Joe was the enigmatic stranger, Marlene the mysterious star; Joe was the androgynous boy to Marlene's ambiguous nymph. They were intrigued and excited by each other.

Joe was one of the few people able to shock Marlene Dietrich. One evening Joe, Dietrich and the American soprano Grace Moore were invited to a formal dinner on the Riviera. When Joe met the other two women in the hotel for cocktails they were horrified to see that she was dressed in men's black tie, and insisted she change into a dress. Shortly afterwards, Joe reappeared in an elegant gown and Dietrich and Moore saw, to their even greater consternation, that her arms were bare and covered with tattoos; she was sent to put back on the tuxedo. Even in this milieu, Joe was outlandish.

Six years later, Remarque used Joe Carstairs as a character in his novel *The Arch of Triumph*, but returned her to her first incarnation, where she sailed in to the cove gleaming and boyish, by rendering her as a man. Dietrich wrote to her husband, 'How do you like Remarque's new book? . . . He paints me worse than I am in order to make everything more interesting, and he succeeds. But everything from Fouquet's to Scheherazade to Antibes, Chateau Madrid, Cherbourg, Lancaster Hotel, even "Jo" on the boat. Of course, he couldn't make it a woman.'

Joe was so infatuated that she offered Whale Cay to Dietrich, population included; Dietrich declined, but accepted a beach. (The deeds to a portion of the island were found in Dietrich's effects after her death.)

When Dietrich and her party returned to America and Joe to the Bahamas after the summer of 1939, the two women continued to see each other. Marlene visited Whale Cay and Joe visited Hollywood. But the friendship soured. After the holiday in France, Marlene decided to employ a companion for her thirteen-year-old daughter. Joe recommended a woman who had worked as her secretary in France. The woman sexually assaulted her young charge. Maria remembered her as a woman whose repulsive masculinity was in striking contrast to Joe's beguiling boyishness:

Although she wore her tailored suits with a skirt and painted the nails of her sausage fingers deep red, this made absolutely no difference to the general effect of – ugly male. With close-set eyes, bulk that overshadowed her pylon legs and very small feet, her resemblance to a rhinoceros was startling. I expected any second her ears to wriggle and a pilot bird to pick insects off her hide.

Dietrich was unaware of the assault at the time, but eventually sacked the woman on suspicion of forging cheques. She was furious with Joe for having introduced her to their lives. She also accused Joe herself of stealing her gem-encrusted bracelet, a gift from Remarque. Joe claimed that Dietrich had given her this bracelet, and one is tempted to believe her, if only because her thefts usually had a comic bent, and she usually boasted about them. On Whale Cay, true to her nickname 'Klep', Joe arranged for one of the servants of the Duke of Windsor to pilfer from Government House the Duke's cigars (for herself) and the Duchess's perfume (for her girlfriends).

Joe later spoke of Dietrich in vitriolic terms: she was 'a wicked old woman, a bitch, not a good person. She was a very stupid woman. No mind, no nothing up there. I don't think she could act, either.' Dietrich had been very shy when she was young, Joe said; as she got older she became 'more flamboyant and nasty'. But, curiously, Joe still described Dietrich as 'the only person who might get me'. On Whale Cay, Joe was the actress, the myth, the icon, the outlaw, the centre of the world. Marlene briefly interrupted that fantasy: Marlene was a star with a wider orbit, a mythic creature of greater power. Joe was jealous.

It was soon after her fling with Dietrich that Carstairs came out of seclusion. She announced her intention to revolutionise the whole of the Bahamian archipelago, befriended the Windsors, wrote poetry, flirted with the idea of starring in films and endeavoured to be a war hero. In 1942 she got the chance to play the brave and benevolent buccaneer.

That August the American ship *Potlatch* was torpedoed off Bird Rock Passage, 350 miles from Nassau, and Carstairs was asked to mount an expedition to find the survivors. Joe sailed out on her rescue mission in the *Vergemere IV*, without the use of lights or radio, through waters known to harbour German U-boats. Dead sailors floated past on the Gulf Stream, their corpses mutilated by sharks. Near Bird Rock Passage, Joe put on the ship's lights and searched the waters. Eventually, she spotted forty-seven American sailors hanging to the deck and sides of a small native schooner. The native boat, too laden down to carry the men to safety, had found the sailors on a deserted island. For thirty days and nights they had lived off sharks, low-flying birds and prickly pears. Many of the men had the fruit's spines in their tongues. All of them were blackened with the sun.

As soon as they boarded the *Vergemere*, the American sailors leapt down the hatches, devoured all the ship's food, and drank most of the water. Several were sick and raving; one had gone mad, and Carstairs and her crew tied him up. A terrible night ensued: the men, some of them on the verge of death, lay about decks awash with diarrhoea. In the morning a few of the sailors asked if they could shave. 'No!' said Joe. 'You've been drinking enough water, you're not going to shave.' 'How about when we get to Nassau?' one asked. 'To hell with that,' Joe replied. 'You can grow your bloody beards.'

They managed to reach Nassau without loss of life, despite the pitching sea and beating sun, to be met by the Daughters of Empire, a group of ladies of the Bahamian establishment headed by the Duchess of Windsor. 'There they were,' said Joe, 'the little white things, all pristine. They weren't properly organised. They didn't have enough stretchers, they didn't have enough ambulances. I was furious.' According to Joe, only when the rescued sailors reached land did they realise that their captain had not been a young man but a forty-two-year-old woman. A year later, the men of the *Potlatch* threw a party in Joe's honour in New York.

In 1943 Joe set up the North Caribbean Transport Company, to carry bananas, ice, sugar and rum from Haiti and Cuba to Miami. Her fleet consisted of *Sonia II*, the schooner spurned by the British and American navies, *Vergemere III* and *Vergemere IV*, the ship built on the island. Many of the cargo ships that usually worked these trade routes had been conscripted by the navy, so Joe's small fleet served a useful purpose. 'It's a sort of war work,' she said. *Sonia* could carry 10,000 stems of bananas at a time, and the many boatloads of sugar ferried by Joe to Nassau were credited with having ended a sugar famine in the Bahamas.

But Joe was poorly rewarded for her heroic rescue of the *Potlatch* sailors or her several attempts to assist the war effort. The people of the islands gossiped about her as if she truly were a treacherous pirate. There were rumours during the war that Joe flew a swastika flag on Whale Cay and that the German U-boats in Bahamian waters were being victualled on her island. The rumours were utterly unfounded. Perhaps they sprang from Joe's tenuous association with Axel Wenner-Gren, to whom she sold vegetables for canning during the war. Wenner-Gren was blacklisted by the Allies for his active links with the Axis powers. The richest living Swede, he had exiled himself to the Bahamas in the 1930s, was a friend of the Windsors, set up businesses on the islands and owned a clutch of cays, several fast motorboats and a huge private yacht (the largest in the world, staffed entirely by pro-Nazi former officers of the Swedish navy). Joe Carstairs and Axel Wenner-Gren did have many things in common, but Nazi sympathies were not among them.

In 1946 Joe sold Bird Cay, two miles from Whale Cay, to her half-brother, Francis Francis. She had bought the island before the war for $8,000, and she turned a huge profit by selling it to Frank for about $150,000. 'Poor Frank,' she said gleefully. On the day she completed the sale she was in high spirits.

An islander whose wife had just given birth to a boy approached her and asked if he could borrow a boat. 'Goddammit,' said Joe. 'You caught me on a good morning. I just sold Bird Cay to my brother. Go to Hutch Lowe and tell him to give you anything you need.' And she handed him a £5 note.

Joe's half-brother Frank had been selected to represent Britain in three Olympic events in 1928, though he had to withdraw after contracting scarlet fever. He had then become a daring aviator and a champion amateur golfer. (Joe dismissed golf, in which both her half-brother and half-sister made their names, as an old person's game.) During the Second World War, Frank helped produce fighter aircraft for the RAF and ferried planes between airfields; he later played a part in inventing the ejection seat. Frank Francis shared Joe's enthusiasm for actresses. In 1929 he had been dismissed from the Royal Horse Guards for marrying an actress, an American named Sunny Jarman; they were later divorced and in 1947 he married another actress, Patricia Leonard.

A year after selling Bird Cay to Frank, Joe was enraged to hear that he was charging his workers to buy vegetables which they had grown, and she turned piratical Robin Hood. One night she mounted a raid on Bird Cay, sending out a posse of men armed with sharpened cutlasses to raze Frank's crops. In effect she was destroying the livelihood of the people she purported to be defending from injustice, but this was clearly secondary to her war with her brother. When the police tried to interview her about the raid she refused to allow them to set foot on her land. In another reprisal attack, in the early 1950s, Joe Carstairs scuttled all her brother's boats, stranding him on his cay. On yet another occasion she and her friends sabotaged Frank's wheat machine by mixing sand with the guinea corn.

These pirate games were partly in the spirit of Arthur Ransome's *Swallows and Amazons* books, in which Nancy Blackett hoists the Jolly Roger above her dinghy, the *Amazon*, to embark on spirited adventures on the waters. But Joe's pranks had a nasty edge. The culture of cruelty in the family was such that Joe would secretly attend amateur golf tournaments in which her half-sister, Sally, was competing and hide in the bushes until the final shot; then she would jump out and shout 'Boo!' to put Sally off her stroke. When Frank visited Whale Cay she played the bossy big sister, sending him and his wife up to their room while one of the party performed a striptease. Frank, in turn, called her Josef (for her resemblance to Stalin), Comtesse (for her marriage to de Pret) or Betty (the name which most irritated her). Once Joe was caught in a storm while sailing in *Little Doctor*, a fishing boat, and she crashed on the shores of Bird Cay. She was forced to seek help from Frank. She refused to admit to any loss of face, merely remarking: 'I managed the boat magnificently.'

Frank distinguished himself as an aircraft pilot before the war, and this may have needled Joe into taking up flying herself: in 1944 she made her first solo flight and the next year won her private pilot's licence. (It was when she looked up her birth certificate, to apply for the licence, that she discovered her mother's real name.) Joe then acquired a Widgeon, a twin-engined plane which cost her $20,000, The plane, importantly, could touch down on water as well as land. 'I understand water better than land,' said Joe. 'I don't have much attraction to land.' Joe flew her plane around the Bahamian archipelago and up to New York.

On one of these journeys, in an episode reminiscent of the descent into the earth at Arras in 1919 and of the plunge into the waters at Detroit in 1928, Joe fell through the sky above Cape Hatteras, and thought she had reached the other world.

She and her co-pilot, a man named Furey, were caught in a terrible storm over North Carolina. The wind was blowing at 80mph and the plane was forced to fly at a dangerous height of 12,000 feet. They were short of oxygen, Furey had a heart condition, and both thought their chances of survival were slim. Suddenly a hole opened in the clouds beneath them. They saw below, lit up by the sun, a disused landing strip and airport. They descended through the clouds, landed and disembarked; canvases flapped around them, and they noticed that the abandoned hangars were filled with birds. As they walked away from the craft they came across a dog who backed off in fear, its hair standing on end. 'Furey, I think we're dead,' Joe said, and the two pinched each other for reassurance. When telling this story, Joe remarked that she and Furey were the same size, could wear each other's clothes almost, and that they must have looked nearly identical in their leather flying jackets. It was a curious aside; it must have passed through Joe's mind that in death she would be twinned with a little man.

The two of them, unsure whether they had been plucked from life or from death, walked on through the deserted landscape until they reached a small store. The people inside looked horrified. 'Now I know we're dead,' Joe told Furey. 'They've seen ghosts.' The storekeeper sold them Coca-Cola and biscuits and told them that they had landed on a former navy airfield. Joe described the incident as 'something to do with a miracle'.

Joe soon hatched ambitious plans for her new hobby. In 1945 she filed for American citizenship and presented the Miami city council with her plan to build a private airport on Lummus Island, to serve the smaller craft which were clogging up the central terminal. The proposed Carstairs Airport was opposed on grounds of the noise and damage to property values it might cause. Joe fought a long battle over planning permission. 'They thought I was an adventurer, an impostor, a bloody foreigner,' she said. A friend asked her if she thought she was the victim of prejudice, as a woman who dressed in men's clothes. 'No, I don't think so,' Joe replied. 'I never thought of it. I've never been conscious of prejudice. Never once.' Joe mounted a vigorous publicity campaign for her airport based on the words 'Progress, Safety, Convenience, Control, Good Citizenship'. In 1948, bitterly, she had to concede defeat. 'It came to the fact that there was not enough money to bribe these fucking people. I refused to do it.'

Ten years later she again crossed swords with the authorities in Miami. *Sealark*, the yacht of a New Orleans businessman, was grounded on a beach at Whale Cay. Joe introduced herself to the owner as the British Commissioner on the island and demanded the surrender of the yacht's papers. He refused to comply so she ran up her own flag, summoned her people and instructed them to loot the yacht; one family took home a television. Joe was subsequently fined $5,000 in the Miami federal court.

If she had been born a boy, Joe said, she would have grown up to be an admiral. Since this was denied her, she turned to piracy. She said that if she had reached the Bahamas a few years earlier, during the American prohibition of alcohol, she would certainly have run rum. 'Oh, rather,' she exclaimed. 'Boy, would I have liked it. I don't give a fuck about the law.' She was tickled by the fact that customs officers often suspected Wadley of being stuffed with contraband. (The *Jack Stripes*, the boat Joe had built to cross the Atlantic in 1928, fulfilled her fantasy for her: in the 1950s, as *Voodoo*, she was said to be the fastest blockade runner in the Mediterranean, ferrying whisky from Tangier to Marseille.)

Joe took her freedom from the sea – she respected its laws more than those of any country, sensed its temperament more keenly than that of any person. 'I don't think anybody knows more about the sea,' she said. 'I understand the sea. Sometimes it's angry, sometimes I'm angry.'

Sea voyages rescued her from her mother when she was eleven and from her country when she was thirty-four. She used to tell people she was born with a caul – with her amniotic sac, the shroud of a miniature sea, wrapped about her head. According to folklore, babies born with a caul were gifted with second sight and immunity from death by drowning; Joe's miraculous escapes in races and storms, then, were evidence of a sea-blessing. To Joe the ocean was a place of flux and metamorphosis. The sea repeatedly baptised her, and she saw herself as a creature of the water rather as Peter Pan was a creature of the air.

18

~~~~~~~~~~

IT FELT LIKE A WOMAN HAD DIED

In Whale Cay Joe had found a home which sur-
passed even an ocean liner – a private world but-
tressed by the water from intruders, surrounded
by a seemingly endless moat. To emphasise the
volume of water that enveloped her, she would tell
visitors to Whale Cay – correctly – that the island
lay not in the Caribbean Sea but at the tongue of the
Atlantic Ocean.

When hurricanes hit Whale Cay the ocean was
whipped from its bed and hurled across the land. Joe
was literally in her element. Among her poems of 1941
was an ode to the hurricane: 'Threshing/ Beating/
Stamping/ Fleeting/ High/ Flying/ Wind/ Of disas-
ter/ Faster/ And faster/ Tear/ Up the world!' In the
summer of 1949 a hurricane blew for twelve hours, the
eye of the storm directly over the island, and reached
150mph. The boards nailed to the windows of the
Great House rattled and slammed. Fish flew across the
sky and fell to lie dying in the roads. The greenhouse

and three houses were quite destroyed. Joe remarked on 'the extraordinary, strange smell that comes, of dampness and dead fish, but to me it was an excitement . . . to me it was delightful.' After the storm the shores of the island lay littered with the carcasses of fish. On one beach the dead fish were swept in and out on the tides for days, and seagulls came down to eat their eyes.

It was a violent hurricane in the late 1940s that drove away Joe's girlfriend Charlotte. Charlotte was classically beautiful, fair, spirited, elegant, charming and, in her own words, 'petted'. They had met in 1941 when Joe – wrapped in a mink coat, her fingernails bright red, her hair coiffed – walked into the bookshop in New York where Charlotte worked. On 1 February, Joe's forty-first birthday and Charlotte's thirty-first, Joe took Charlotte on a drive round Central Park in a limousine, plied her with Aquavit, presented her with a Cartier bracelet and invited her to Whale Cay. Charlotte accepted.

In the early 1940s the island was at its most vibrant – a hive of activity, agricultural and social, with guests arriving for parties by the boatload. Charlotte loved the fun of Whale Cay and enjoyed helping to run the Great House. She thought Joe hilarious and magnificent. But increasingly she found island life too rugged and lonely; the hurricane turned out to be the last straw. Charlotte admitted also that, though she adored Joe, in the end she was 'too rich fare'.

Charlotte detected a sadness in Joe: there was something missing, she said, and this something was bound up in Wadley. 'She had the heart of a child,' Charlotte wrote, and, enigmatically: 'She could charm the birds off the trees – but it wasn't the birds she was after.'

Joe's girlfriends had to be good-looking and they had to be young, but that apart there was no discernible pattern to the women with whom she chose to live. From 1950 there was Jackki, a gregarious, bossy red-haired New Yorker in her early twenties. 'Crazy and adorable,' said Joe. When they met, Jackki was working as a manicurist in Miami, at a beauty salon that Joe visited to have the tips of her hair singed and her fingernails cut and buffed. One evening Jackki left work to find that her car had vanished and in its place was a brand-new Chevrolet, a gift from Joe. This was the opening gambit of a determined courtship, and Jackki was soon persuaded to move to Whale Cay. Jackki was an energetic organiser, remembered by many islanders for her thoughtfulness – she took a keen interest in the welfare of children on the island and was instrumental in setting up the Star of the Bahamas camp.

Jackki shared Joe's relish for mischief and adventure. When Joe heard that a friend in Miami was having the chief of the local fire brigade to dinner, she made a hoax call reporting a fire at her friend's house. She and Jackki hid in the bushes outside to watch the scene of confusion when the engine roared up. In the early 1950s the two went on safari to Kenya with the composer Bart Howard's friend Bud; it was twenty years since Joe had hunted game in India with another manicurist, Mabs Jenkins. The holiday in Africa, though, was a disaster, because Bud shot a lion and Joe did not. Joe returned furious.

After Jackki there was Jorie, otherwise known as Chop, a shy black woman twenty-four years Joe's junior. Joe said Jorie was 'one of the nicest people I have ever known' – and 'unbelievably exciting'. They met at a New York poker party, and in 1957 Jorie, who had never before lived with a woman, left the bank at which she worked to join Joe on Whale Cay. By then the island population had shrunk to about 100. Jorie was a tomboy and she threw herself into all Joe's ventures – she worked hard helping to run the island and she loved to go out in the boats. On Whale Cay, Joe said, Jorie 'went from being someone who slept eighteen hours a day to someone very vital . . . she came to life.' Joe pointed out that Jorie was thirty-four when she moved to the island, exactly the age Joe had been. Jorie afforded her a vicarious rebirth.

One day in the late 1950s a sudden pain in the legs tore through Joe Carstairs's invulnerability, and she let out a piercing scream from her room in the Great House on Whale Cay, an involuntary mortal – and feminine – cry. The servants concocted a potion (of her own urine and crushed leaves) to soothe her limbs. Though she had spent her life endeavouring to ignore it, Joe Carstairs was made of flesh and blood.

Joe was for the next three decades to be assailed by reminders of her mortality. Her hair turned white and her body began to malfunction. She did her best to put a manly gloss on her ailments. She claimed, improbably, that her teeth were falling out because of the poor diet she had been forced to adopt in Ireland during the First World War. As the problems with her legs worsened, she said the aches and pains were caused by a hip injury sustained in a motorboat crash (in fact only her ribs had been damaged in her racing days, and the doctors – to her fury – attributed her pains to arthritis). When she was finally persuaded to undergo a hip operation she was eager to point out that the surgeon 'did a lot of footballers'.

Just as she resisted mortality, Joe wanted to believe herself, like Wadley, immune to social and historical forces. To a great extent, her money ensured that she was. When a friend remarked in the 1970s that times had changed she retorted, 'You bet they have – not my times, though.' Yet, by one reading at least, the movements of her life closely followed shifts in public attitudes: she threw herself into the limelight in the naughty Twenties, went into exile in the reproving Thirties, came out again during the Second World War (when manly qualities in women were briefly acceptable), returned to exile in its aftermath, and when she finally rejoined the wider world in the Sixties it was in part because times had again changed, and her brand of colonialism had had its day.

Black Bahamians achieved a degree of emancipation and independence in the 1960s, and the islanders remaining on Whale Cay became increasingly disrespectful towards 'the Boss'. The Reverend Prince Hepburn said that Joe asked him on three occasions to come over from Nassau to deal with women on the island who were getting drunk and hollering abuse at the Great House. 'Instead of coming out and talking to your helpers,' shouted Miss Martha, Joe's favourite laundress, 'you are in there sweethearting your women just like you.' Each time, Hepburn said, he evicted the troublemakers from the island. It was a sad sign of Joe's declining power that she felt unequal to dealing with trouble on Whale Cay herself. She was no longer able to control the behaviour of her people. While walking across the island one day she was appalled to find a couple copulating under a coconut palm just off the main road.

Joe spent less and less time on Whale Cay. Instead she sailed to Miami on the *St Pete*, a naval supply vessel which she had converted to a houseboat. This floating home, moored in a quiet stretch of the Miami river, was a private island in miniature. Protected from the gossip of neighbours, Joe and Jorie lived there together for a time. The two would go out to nightclubs and parties, sometimes not returning to the boat until the early hours. Joe had a scare in the 1960s when she left Wadley on the *St Pete* one night and returned to find the boat had been burgled. 'I should never have left him there,' she said, and added: 'There were a lot of fingermarks on him but they didn't do anything to him. Wadley has frightened people, in a funny way.' Her authority may have been weakened, but Wadley was as powerful as ever.

Joe of course never admitted to any humiliation on Whale Cay. She eventually decided to leave the island, she said, because of the growth in drug trafficking in the Bahamas; the Berry Islands were a convenient stopping point on the route to Miami. Joe said she decided she had to get out before she was provoked into shooting someone. And besides, *St Pete*, on which she commuted from the island, 'began to get sick and old'.

In 1975 Joe sold Whale Cay, for just under $1 million, and for the second time in her life she cried: 'It felt like a woman had died.'

'I could've gone out and shot myself,' Joe said. She was convinced that, without her, the island would wilfully revert to wilderness. 'It wants to go back,' she said. *Estelle IV*, her favourite racing boat, had been consigned to the bottom of a river on the island – 'I left her there, to die.'

The pain of leaving was so great that Joe could not

afterwards bear to see beaches and rocks pictured on television. 'I've become an absolute coward,' she admitted. 'I can't face it. I can't look something in the face that I've left behind.' 'Whale Cay was really a part of her,' said Jorie.

In the trauma of parting from the island, Joe threw much of her emotion on to the objects around her. She noted that the house she moved into in Miami 'put itself out to please me in every way'; it 'did its bit', and at nights she would assure it aloud, 'I love you, house.' Joe took with her every stick of furniture from Whale Cay, and did not buy anything new. The penguins came too: 'I don't think they really know that there was any transition,' she said. Friends thought it a peculiarly English, even Victorian, trait that she garnered and kept so much memorabilia. Joe displayed the photographs of her girlfriends – some 120 in all – on a glass-topped table. 'There were one or two, of course,' she remarked, 'that I liked apart from sex.'

A friend of hers once reflected on how wonderful it was to love and be loved. 'I don't know what you're talking about,' Joe said. 'I don't love people.' Some of this was bravado. Joe's girlfriends remembered her as extremely affectionate and romantic. She was also loyal, and never cut her ties with anyone for whom she had cared. But she did her best to dispense with feelings of love or pain. 'Smile,/ Loves of my forgotten nights,'

Joe wrote in one of her poems, 'Now just a series/ In my mind – / Why have you yet to learn/ That love is just a phase,/ To laugh,/ And turn your face/ Away from time!'

Jorie, Charlotte and Jackki all eventually left Joe to take up relationships with other women – or at least that was the way they saw it. 'Usually I dumped them because I got tired of them,' said Joe. 'I did it in various ways, rather devious, so they didn't realise they were being pushed.' In other words, she imagined that unbeknown to her girlfriends she engineered their decisions to leave. Joe framed events so that she was always the protagonist, never had to feel herself inadequate or abandoned.

From 1976 until 1990 Joe lived in Florida and spent the summers in Sag Harbor and Water Mill, Long Island. At Water Mill she entertained the local nuns to tea. All her homes were near the sea, and her menagerie of objects came to include a number of model whales, in remembrance of Whale Cay. Joe liked to go on whale-watching expeditions off Sag Harbor.

Carstairs carried around her suffering and her memories in objects instead of in her head or heart. She was very particular about the arrangement of her things: all the stuffed toys, pictures of boats, the chairs and tables had a place. Women posed the greatest threat to this order. 'No *woman* has ever tried to rearrange my house,' she said. 'Lots of women try to change furniture. It's a thing they do – it's a deplorable trait. All women do it.'

The kernel of her baggage was Wadley. And he had his own baggage – a miniature cheque-book, a wallet, a plastic castle, a cigar case, cufflinks, tie-pins, a wristwatch that ticked, revolvers, golf clubs, a Bible, books of poetry, a dog, and his own dolls. Wadley, she noted with delight in 1976, 'still looks like a boy . . . He's 51 now – he will be this Christmas – and he's still got that boyish look.' Wadley was a deeply benign influence, Joe believed. He was a model of good behaviour: abstemious, uncomplaining, seen but not heard, he served as a moral example, a tamer of base instincts. Joe admitted that she only had to look at Wadley's sweet face for a fit of temper to subside. 'I'm quite sure I would have been a different person if it hadn't been for him,' she said. 'He's extraordinary what he does for me.'

If she invested objects with emotion, Joe could also seem to have replaced her emotions with objects. It was said sometimes that she had a cheque-book where her heart ought to be – she responded to sickness in others not with sentiment but with offers of money (and often opined that they would be better off dead). Her kindnesses always took material form, the currency in her friendships became her wealth. All the girlfriends with whom she lived remained close to her, tied to her with ropes of money as well as affection.

'Nobody became my enemy,' she said. 'Not one.' If anyone spurned her money, Joe felt herself spurned. Bart Howard, who visited Whale Cay in the 1940s, recalled that his friendship with Joe never recovered from his decision to pay his own air fare to the Bahamas. 'She'd lost me, sort of. She was never so nice to me. She liked being able to do something for me.'

In the late 1980s Joe was providing annual incomes for former girlfriends such as Charlotte, Jackki and Jorie; for relatives of former girlfriends, including Ruth Baldwin's sister; and for a number of former employees and their families. 'It is the only proper way to behave,' she maintained. People said she had a heart of gold. Yet these financial ties meant Joe could never be sure her friendships would survive on affection alone. She had to have a heart as hard as gold, because she could not fully trust anyone – except Wadley. It was part of this doll's magic that he remained untouched by her wealth.

'We're like one,' Joe said. 'He's me and I'm him. It's a marvellous thing. If everybody had a Wadley there'd be less sadness in the world.'

19

~~~~~~~~

ONLY WADLEY

As Joe Carstairs aged and slowed, she and Wadley swapped places. Where Wadley had been the innocent and Joe the rogue, he was now the playboy. Wadley, Joe said, had taken to drinking brandy, smoking cigars and playing poker. She claimed that he consorted with Jack Kennedy in the early 1960s. 'You know, Wadley was friendly with him, in a funny way,' Joe said. 'They went to the Bay of Pigs together . . . He had a *tremendous* liking for him.' In 1967 Wadley landed on the moon with the American astronauts, and one of Joe's girlfriends made a painting commemorating Wadley's space voyage.

While Joe started to describe herself as an 'it', as if she were turning into a doll, Wadley — like Jack Kennedy — became sexually voracious. Despite the fact he had at least one wife (Wadley married in the 1920s and again in the 1940s), he had scores of doll girlfriends. Many of these were gifts exchanged

between Joe and her former lovers and some —
including three redheaded girl dolls belonging to
one redheaded woman — had to be kept away from
Wadley to save him from temptation. Wadley even
started to breed.

'Being a man, he had a lot of babies,' Joe said.
'And we used to have to pay for that.' Only one of
Wadley's offspring bore his name. In the late 1970s
Ann Azzara, an energetic woman of Irish descent
who was married to a New York Italian, struck up
a friendship with Joe Carstairs; the older woman's
tales of adventure on the seas reminded Ann, she
said, of the stories her father used to tell. Ann had
learnt to cook on board her father's ship and she
would make ship's breakfasts for Joe: marmalade,
toast, kippers, herrings and mushrooms. Ann was
enchanted by Wadley. When she became pregnant, Joe
announced: 'Wadley did it. Cad-dad did it.' Ann's baby
was named Daniel Tod Wadley Azzara, and when he
was seven Joe taught him to smoke Wadley's cigars.

In the 1980s Joe embarked with some friends
on a property venture in New York, and dubbed
the company Wadley Associates: its stationery was
imprinted with the Wadley crown. Her philanthropic
gestures, too, became firmly associated with Wadley.
In the 1980s she introduced him to the sons of her
tailor in Long Island, aged four and five. Wadley was
dressed elegantly, like an English gentleman, and with

him was a bodyguard, a little black boy with a golden gun. 'I'll tell you a secret,' Joe said to the boys. 'Wadley is very rich. See his gold chain? If you're very good, one day he'll be good to you.' Every Christmas Wadley would give toys to the tailor's boys, and through her he set up a fund for them to be educated at college. To another little boy of her acquaintance Joe gave an Acme Thunderer whistle, with a note attached: 'Merry Christmas to my pal from Tod Wadley. Always whistle when you need someone or something.' If asked what she wanted as a gift, Joe would reply, 'I don't really need anything – get something for Wadley.'

In 1978 Joe asked Hugh Harrison, a handsome man of about sixty who she had met on Long Island, to move in with her. 'I've had it with these fucking women,' she said. To prove that she was serious, she said he could bring his cat, Bean (cats, of course, were abhorrent to Joe). Hugh had taken to Joe instantly and he accepted her offer. He stayed with her as a friend and paid companion until she died. They lived first in Miami and then in Naples, a well-heeled resort on the west coast of Florida. Joe's house in Naples was another mock-ship, with solid wooden walls, cathedral ceilings, and the sea on the doorstep. It was lit, like the house on Whale Cay, with copper ship's lanterns. Joe lived there with Hugh, Bean, a cook, a maid and, as she became more debilitated, a succession of nurses. Bean soon learned that her bedroom was out-of-bounds.

When Joe had an operation for cataracts, she was delighted at the excuse to don a jaunty black eye-patch. She recalled with relish that in the 1920s she had been wearing just such a piratical patch, and a naval officer's overcoat, when an old man had mistaken her for a boy and tried to pick her up at Berlin railway station. Ever insistent on her virility, Joe would return from a drive and announce that she and Samson (her car) had raced another car at more than 100mph. She would stride into a room full of strangers, her skin tough and tanned, her hair cropped and white, and comment loudly on it being 'fuck-awful cold' before rolling up her sleeves to reveal her wrinkled tattoos. On one arm was the scar from a game she had played on Whale Cay in 1950: she and a woman named Betsy had engaged in a competition to see who could hold a burning cigarette to their skin for longest. 'I was young,' Joe explained. 'Fifty . . . Just a child, just a child.'

Joe complained that people were more energetic when she was young. Now there were 'dope fiends' everywhere, with their 'blank, stary eyes'. Maybe she was haunted by the blank, stary eyes of the drug addicts of her youth: her mother, her first idol (Dolly Wilde) and her first love (Ruth Baldwin). Even when in pain, Joe resisted taking any kind of drug. Her doctor, seeing that her spirits were low, suggested that he prescribe Prozac. 'I don't take medicine,' she snapped.

Joe liked to watch boxing on television; George Foreman was her favourite, and she greeted his appearances with 'There's my George.' She also watched videos: swashbuckling adventures starring the likes of Errol Flynn; films which involved shooting animals in India or Africa; films about maritime disasters, such as the sinking of the *Titanic*; and *Jaws*: 'Oh, how I loved *Jaws*,' said Joe. 'I liked him – the shark.' She enjoyed anything featuring David Niven, whom she thought she resembled in her staunch and elegant Englishness. Joe's favourite blazer bore a British crest and golden buttons bought in the 1920s. She used to bemoan the loss of British power and prestige, especially in the former colonies: 'England's gone down the drain, dammit!'

And Joe watched videotapes of Dietrich films. She effected a kind of reconciliation with Marlene when she went to one of her concerts in Miami and then sought an audience with the star backstage. 'She kissed me,' Joe said afterwards.

As she got older, Joe lived more and more simply, and talked mockingly of the 'rich kids' who lived in Naples. She had always shunned conspicuous displays of wealth. She used money in strictly functional ways: to build boats, to shoot animals, to buy cars, to run an island, to dress smartly, to keep the house clean, to provide for her friends and workers. If she could not use her money to build and make, she barely spent any on herself at all. Some things were worth spending on, though. In the late 1980s Joe donated her racing trophies to the newly opened National Motorboat Museum at Pitsea, Essex. She paid for their shipping to England and for a bullet-proof cabinet to house them. (When the museum came to insure the trophies, it discovered that they were not the silver-plated originals, but solid silver copies cast after the house at Mulberry Walk was burgled in the 1930s.)

Joe inspired love in those she used her money to 'look after'. While living in Miami on the *St Pete* she met a man who had idolised her since the First World War. William O'Brien, or 'Obie', was serving in the Coldstream Guards in 1917 when he read an article in the *News of the World* which described Joe's work as an ambulance driver in France. He cut out the article and carried it with him for years, even after emigrating to Florida. In the 1920s he read with pride of her motorboating victories and in the 1960s was overwhelmed finally to run into his hero. Joe employed him as a boat mechanic and gave him a sailor-doll. Obie called Joe 'The Skipper'. After her death he wrote: 'I have lived and worked for her boats . . . and I have always loved her.'

When Joe left Long Island for good in the late 1980s she offered to provide an income for her tailor, Joe

Visone, and his wife, 'Mrs Joe'. The Visones declined the offer. 'I don't want it,' Joe Visone told Joe Carstairs. 'I want you.' Her friends too repaid her generosity with love. After the war, Bardie Coleclough lived apart from her husband, Air Vice Marshal Sir William Tyrrell, surgeon to the King. She became a Communist, a CND activist and a maniacal vegetarian and Rolls-Royce enthusiast. The money Joe sent her each year safeguarded her independence. In 1986, the year she died aged eighty-nine, Bardie wrote to Joe: 'You have given me freedom. I miss you still and forever Klep.'

Joe's world, though, was increasingly peopled with her dolls. As a present for Joe, Hugh Harrison sent off for a 'Mea Doll', whose blank face was superimposed with a photograph of the face of its owner. Joe Carstairs kissed the face of her Mea Doll so fervently that it became rubbed away and smeared with red lipstick; another doll in Joe's image was sent for, in case the face of the first vanished completely. Friends of Joe gave the twin Mea Dolls gifts – tennis racquets and sweatshirts emblazoned with the letter 'W' for Wimbledon – and the pair became known as the Tennis Boys. Then there were other dolls, together a silent spectacle of Joe's fantasies: the Chinaman, the cowboy with his horse, the golliwog, the guardsman, the old man, the sailor boys. Many had talismanic qualities – on occasion Joe was given toy elephants,

"TO MY DARLING JOE"

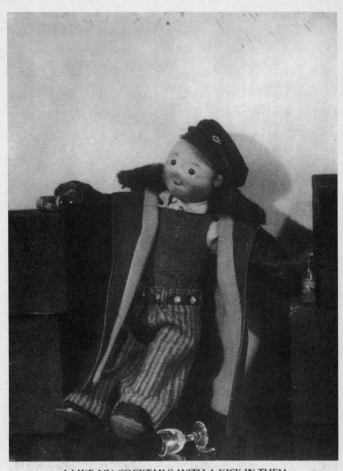

I LIKE MY COCKTAILS WITH A KICK IN THEM

I INTERVIEW THE PRESS IN MY BATH

OF COURSE, GARY COOPER IS A BACK NUMBER NOW

LOVE AT FIRST SIGHT

WEDDED BLISS

GOODBYE TO ALL THAT

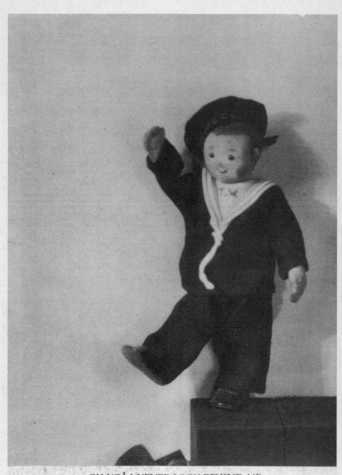

OH NO! I NEVER LOOK BEHIND ME

but she refused to accept them unless their trunks were erect, pointing upwards 'for luck'.

Towards the end, Joe changed her will at least twice a year, carefully charting out her relationships in the language of cash and possessions – in total, some sixty-eight versions were drawn up. In her final will, she shared the bulk of her fortune – about $33 million before tax – between Hugh, Charlotte, Jackki, Jorie and her girlfriend, John Howcroft and his wife, and Dorothy Edwards, the secretary of Joe's lawyer. In addition, she made more than thirty individual bequests to friends and employees, ranging from $5,000 to $600,000 and totalling about $2,500,000. She made specific bequests of the most precious of her possessions.

Jackki was given, among other things, 'my large black wooden elephant, my silver jug, my gold plaque with sun emblem, my large natural bear and pillow of Wadley which is on my bed'. Hugh was to have 'my two Mea dolls, my two handmade wooden chairs in the Florida room together with my two needlepoint pillows, the raccoon in the chair in my room, my plate in the frame in my room, my two stuffed boy dolls, my soft yellow dog with the long fuzzy tail, my large and small tortoises and my ceramic yellow and spotted dogs'.

Joe left John Howcroft, who had helped run Whale Cay in the early days, 'my ceramic sea gull and wooden ship, both of which are on the piano in the living-room, my stuffed dog John, the stuffed dog in the chair in my bedroom, the picture of my ship which is in my room and my bronze of Wadley'. To Ann Azzara went 'my large leather penguin which is in the Florida room, my book on Lord Tod Wadley and my framed poem about Wadley, both of which are in my bedroom'. (The book on Tod Wadley consisted of photographs and captions.)

Doris Cook, Joe's housekeeper in Naples, was allocated 'my stuffed bear with eye shade, two old men, one of whom is on a horse, my stuffed soldier and camel and any other stuffed animals and dolls that she may want, other than those specifically bequeathed herein'.

All personal property not identified in the will could be distributed at the executor's discretion – except the toys. Joe inserted a clause to this effect. 'I direct my Executor to make such distribution as he may believe I would wish of my furniture and other tangible personal property wherever located which is not hereinabove effectively bequeathed to other beneficiaries . . . excepting however that all stuffed animals and dolls which are not specifically bequeathed or taken by Doris Cook shall be burned.'

Joe boasted of having outlived her younger brother and sister – Sally and Frank both died in the 1980s – and placed bets on the fact she would live to ninety-four. She had terrific rows with Hugh over which of them was the more manly (he was gay, a fact that she used against him). '*She* sure doesn't mellow,' Hugh remarked. But in truth the fight was going out of her and sometimes after a bruising exchange Joe would sit repeating to herself, 'I never cry, I'll never cry, I never cry, I'll never cry.' If she was upset she would huddle with Wadley in her bed. She liked Hugh to address each furry toy and doll in turn when he came to her bedroom to say goodnight; Joe replied on their behalf. 'Goodnight, Tennis Boys.' 'Goodnight, Hugh.' 'Goodnight, Raccoon.' 'Goodnight, Hugh.'

Joe began to refer to her limbs as detached and insensible, as pieces of meat. Her legs were legs of lamb, then mutton. 'Let's put mutton to bed,' she would say to her nurse; she sent out money to earthquake victims, and speculated on the possibility of cooking up her mutton legs to give to the poor. Her substitute limbs, in turn, came to life. Joe Carstairs called her walking frame 'Spider' (it bore a sign with its name) and her walking sticks 'my two boys'.

Joe became terrified that somebody might hurt Wadley, and sometimes would withdraw from an argument for Wadley's sake, afraid that her adversary might damage him in anger. She once went back to her car to fetch Wadley on a sunny day, in case he was uncomfortably hot. More realistically, she had a horror of moths.

And Wadley did decay. His beady eyes remained

bright but his leather face darkened and split. Soon it was plastered with tiny band-aids. 'I know he's old,' Joe said. 'He's an old dolly, bless his heart, but my God he's still got that boyish smile and look.' Once, when Wadley's arm was damaged, Joe sent him to a toy-mender. But she could not bear to be separated from him for long, and after a sleepless night sent for him to be returned at dawn.

'You never really needed anybody,' a friend said to her.

'Only Wadley,' Joe replied.

'What would you do if something happened to Wadley?'

'No,' Joe said quickly. 'I don't want to consider it.'

Her friend persisted. 'What would you do if you were driving your car and . . .' Joe interrupted sharply. 'No. I don't want to talk about it.'

A woman who encountered Lord Tod Wadley in the 1980s was disturbed by the doll, could not shake him from her mind for days. 'He looks so lively,' she said, and then, 'like something dead'. Instead of transcending life and death, Wadley oscillated between them, uncannily.

As Joe's body slowly gave out she took comfort from the fact that she was shrinking: 'I'll be Wadley-size when I die.' Maybe, at last, she was becoming a boy-doll. To sustain the illusion, Joe guarded her privacy: even at her weakest, she would not let her nurse wash the front of her body. When she became incontinent, the nurse provided her with waterproof underwear. 'They make these for men, don't they?' said Joe. 'Get those.'

She discouraged friends from visiting because she could not stand for them to see her ill. But she did not neglect her appearance. Joe loved to have her hair brushed, would not leave her bedroom without being properly dressed, and even before going to the bathroom put on foundation and lipstick – a bright red streak. 'I look good,' she would say. 'I know. I can't hear, I can't see, but I look good.'

Joe fell into a coma on 18 December 1993, a few weeks short of her ninety-fourth birthday. As she lay unconscious, her nurse placed Wadley in her arms and gently brushed her hair. The nurse whispered to Joe that it was 9.40, hoping that if she heard the words nine and four she might believe she had reached the age of ninety-four, the hour she had appointed for her death.

Joe died that night. The cat Bean knew when she was gone: he strolled into her room for the first time and sat near the head of the bed to watch her. In the morning a man from the undertakers' came for Joe's body. His name was Todd.

Wadley and Joe were cremated together. Their ashes, with those of Ruth Baldwin, were taken from

Florida to Long Island, where a memorial service was held in a Presbyterian whalers' church. As a souvenir for the mourners, Jackki had photographs of Joe and Wadley spliced together. The two are reproduced at the same height, but Wadley's bulk is such that he is a giant to Joe's elf. The remains of Joe, Wadley and Ruth were placed in a tomb near the sea.

When I was completing this book, more than two years after Joe Carstairs's death, I again visited her goddaughter Jane Harrison-Hall. She asked after Lord Tod Wadley and I told her he had been cremated.

'Oh! that saddens me,' said Mrs Harrison-Hall. 'Poor Wadley. How could she?'

UNTITLED

The human touch
Is often disappointing
Although I cannot say
I've suffered much
I still maintain
That friendship
Should be true and loyal
And rare
And so
I've chosen one
Whose brown-eyed stare
Is straight
And undeceptive
He is always
On my side
Although he doesn't
'Yes' me
His quiet
And unobtrusive ways
Are such
That boredom
Never enters in
My praise of him
Is such

That if I ever

Dared begin

To phrase

My praise

Its echo

Would not cease

To ring

And so

To cut this story short

I'll tell you all

He's only 13 inches tall

Half doll

Half boy

Half real

Half toy

My mascot

Lord Tod Wadley

M. B. Carstairs, circa 1955

NOTES

Among the books I have used in research are *The Story of the Bahamas* by Paul Albury, *Nightwood* by Djuna Barnes, *In Memory of Dorothy Ierne Wilde* edited by Natalie Clifford Barney, *Peter Pan* by J. M. Barrie, *Smouldering Wood and The Winding Stair* by Hans Jacob Bernstein, *Tallulah Bankhead* by Jeffrey L. Carrier, *Lot's Wife: Lesbian Paris 1890–1914* by Catherine van Casselaer, *The Rockefellers* by Peter Collier and David Horowitz, *Powerboat Speed* by Kevin Desmond, *Odd Girls and Twilight Lovers* by Lillian Faderman, *Djuna: the formidable Miss Barnes* by Andrew Field, *No Man's Land* by Sandra M. Gilbert and Susan Gubar, *The Monkey Gland Affair* by David Hamilton, *Sacred Cowes* by Anthony Heckstall-Smith, *Serious Pleasures* by Philip Hoare, *John D. Rockefeller* by Silas Hubbard, *Who Killed Harry Oakes?* by Michael Leasor, *Every Other Inch a Lady* by Beatrice Lillie, *The White Witch of Rosehall* by Herbert George de Lisser, *Ten, Ten, the Bible Ten: Obeah in the Bahamas* by

Timothy McCartney, *The King over the Water* by Michael Pye, *Fast Boats and Flying Boats* by Adrian Rance, *Arch of Triumph* by Erich Maria Remarque, *Marlene Dietrich* by Maria Riva, *Bahamian Society after Emancipation* by Gail Saunders, *Motor Boats* by F. Strickland, *Loving Garbo* by Hugo Vickers, *Rejuvenation by Grafting* by Serge Voronoff, *Speed: the authentic life of Sir Malcolm Campbell* by J. Wentworth Day, *Amazons and Military Maids* by Julie Wheelwright, *Orlando* by Virginia Woolf, and the memoirs of Molly Coleclough, John Edward Johnston-Noad and Joan Mackern. Thanks to the Estate of Bettina Bergery, c/o P. S. Thacher, Stonington, CT, USA, for permission to quote from Bettina Bergery's contribution to *In Memory of Dorothy Ierne Wilde* on pages 31 and 32. The photograph of Joe on the frontispiece and that of Helen Volck were kindly provided by the Estate of George Platt Lynes; the photograph of Joe in the Museum at Whale Cay by D. Scherman/Life/Katz; and the photograph of the unknown woman on a beach by Philippe Halsman/Magnum. The photographs not credited individually were provided either by friends (see below) or courtesy of the Estate of Joe Carstairs.

Most of the stories in this book were provided by those who knew Joe Carstairs, as were the photographs and tape-recordings I have used. For their help and generosity, many thanks to Esther Albury, Myrlyn Allen, Victor Azzara, Katja Beck, Nicolette Bethel, Ernest Callendar, Claudine Callendar, Bradley Callendar, Julie

Canavan, Peter Chester, Doris Cook, Margaret Craft, Kevin Desmond, Mary Donahue, Eileen Dupuch, Rivers Fletcher, Patricia Francis, Vanessa Francis, Jane Harrison-Hall, Madeleine Harrison-Hall, Hilton Harvey, Irene Harvey, the Reverend Prince Hepburn, Mary Hinck, Bart Howard, John Jessup, Major Gerald Leonard, Bill Lightbourne, Muriel Lightbourne, Anna Nemec, the late William O'Brien, Crofton Peddie, Doris Pratt, Maria Riva, Peter Riva, Eric See, Oliver Sinnicks, Caroline Skeates, Binney Slater, Betty Thompson, Joe Visone, Emmanuela Visone, William Wong and Bachoo Woronzow. Special thanks to Hugh Harrison, and to Kim Aranha, Marjorie Austin, Ann Azzara, Dorothy Edwards, Charlotte Landau and Jacqueline Rae.

My thanks to Kate Goodhart, Charlotte Greig and Joanna Prior at Fourth Estate, London, and to Kathryn Court and Laurie Walsh at Viking Penguin, New York. For their ideas and encouragement, many thanks also to Will Cohu, Hugh Massingberd, Susan Feldman, Claudia FitzHerbert, Eric Bailey, Matt Seaton, Ruth Picardie, Wycliffe Stutchbury, Tamsin Currey, David Jones, Stephen O'Connell, Daniel Nogues, Eileen Vizard, Ann Dowker, Ian Parker, John Pitcher, Kathy O'Shaughnessy and — especially — to Miranda Fricker, Keith Wilson and Valerie, Juliet and Ben Summerscale. Thanks most of all to Christopher Potter, my editor, to David Miller, my agent, and to Robert Randall.

FOR THE BEST IN PAPERBACKS, LOOK FOR THE

In every corner of the world, on every subject under the sun, Penguin represents quality and variety—the very best in publishing today.

For complete information about books available from Penguin—including Puffins, Penguin Classics, and Arkana—and how to order them, write to us at the appropriate address below. Please note that for copyright reasons the selection of books varies from country to country.

In the United Kingdom: Please write to *Dept. EP, Penguin Books Ltd, Bath Road, Harmondsworth, West Drayton, Middlesex UB7 0DA.*

In the United States: Please write to *Penguin Putnam Inc., P.O. Box 12289 Dept. B, Newark, New Jersey 07101-5289* or call 1-800-788-6262.

In Canada: Please write to *Penguin Books Canada Ltd, 10 Alcorn Avenue, Suite 300, Toronto, Ontario M4V 3B2.*

In Australia: Please write to *Penguin Books Australia Ltd, P.O. Box 257, Ringwood, Victoria 3134.*

In New Zealand: Please write to *Penguin Books (NZ) Ltd, Private Bag 102902, North Shore Mail Centre, Auckland 10.*

In India: Please write to *Penguin Books India Pvt Ltd, 11 Panchsheel Shopping Centre, Panchsheel Park, New Delhi 110 017.*

In the Netherlands: Please write to *Penguin Books Netherlands bv, Postbus 3507, NL-1001 AH Amsterdam.*

In Germany: Please write to *Penguin Books Deutschland GmbH, Metzlerstrasse 26, 60594 Frankfurt am Main.*

In Spain: Please write to *Penguin Books S. A., Bravo Murillo 19, 1° B, 28015 Madrid.*

In Italy: Please write to *Penguin Italia s.r.l., Via Benedetto Croce 2, 20094 Corsico, Milano.*

In France: Please write to *Penguin France, Le Carré Wilson, 62 rue Benjamin Baillaud, 31500 Toulouse.*

In Japan: Please write to *Penguin Books Japan Ltd, Kaneko Building, 2-3-25 Koraku, Bunkyo-Ku, Tokyo 112.*

In South Africa: Please write to *Penguin Books South Africa (Pty) Ltd, Private Bag X14, Parkview, 2122 Johannesburg.*